ACCLAIM FOR RUSSIA BY RIVER

"An excellent and entertaining account of cruising the Volga and its tributaries."
  – *St. Petersburg Press*

"*Russia by River* uses candor and humor to paint a realistic picture of both Russia's volatile present and its turbulent past."
  – *Porthole Magazine*

"An invaluable primer on river cruising in Russia."
  – *San Diego Union Tribune*

"With this book the traveler has detailed descriptions of all the stops along the way...plus insider info on seeing the hidden side of Russia."
  – *Access Russia*

"It gave us a clearer understanding of what we were seeing."
  – *International Travel News*

"The most helpful guide I had in Russia. No other one was needed."
  – Judith T. Bowles, Ventura, CA

"It is far superior as a day-to-day guide to any other book...."
  – Shirley Rae Don, Harrisburg, PA

"Of all the information I looked up before and after the trip, I found *Russia by River* more complete."
  – Frank Elmgren, Austin, TX

"Comprehensive and fascinating to peruse."
  – Rafael and Dolores Moreu, Longwood, FL

"The book has made a tremendous contribution to my trip...."
  – W. J. Tack, The Netherlands

"Bravo and thank you to the author!"
  – François Motte, Roubaix, France

Russia by River

The Moscow–St. Petersburg Cruise

by
howard shernoff

RIVER CRUISE PROMOTIONS, INC.

ABOUT THE AUTHOR

Howard Shernoff, born in California, is known as the guru of Russian river cruising. When Howard joined the staff of the MS *Russ* in 1993, he was the first American to work on a Russian passenger ship. He remained in Russia for seven more years, residing in St. Petersburg and cruising the rivers annually. Howard is also the author of the *River Cruise Phrasebook* and of *China by River: The Yangtze River Cruise*. He travels widely and frequently and resides in Tallinn, Estonia.

SPECIAL THANKS

To MS *Russ* Cruise Director Zina Petrashova for giving me the opportunity to live Russia by River before writing it; to former MS *Surkov* First Chartman Gennadiy Matveyev for spending cold marathon sessions with me in front of navigational maps; to Jennifer Mitchell for running the business, taking photos, conducting research and proofing the proofs; to Sergey Selivanov for keeping things afloat in St. Petersburg; and to my brother and creative partner Mitchell for being a meaningful part of this publication and all that I undertake.

Photographs by Howard Shernoff and Jennifer Mitchell
Cover design, maps and photo digitization by Mitchell Shernoff

Published by River Cruise Promotions Inc. in the United States of America
www.rivercruisepromotions.com
ISBN 0-9705300-0-5

Be sure to visit Russia by River on the Internet at www.russiabyriver.com
Send your feedback to cruise@russiabyriver.com

CONTENTS

INTRODUCTION

Ever since its first publication in 1994, *Russia by River* has remained the only comprehensive insider guide dedicated exclusively to the Moscow–St. Petersburg river cruise. It is, by all accounts, an indispensable companion for the journey. Without it, you must rely on infrequent onboard announcements to figure out where you are and what you are seeing. With it, you transcend from the plight of dumbfounded tourist to the status of enlightened traveler. Plus you possess a handy keepsake of your voyage.

The book documents practically every point of interest, landmark and village lying along the 1,400-kilometer-long river route. But that's not all. It provides succinct yet complete information on all ports of call, including Moscow and St. Petersburg, as well as on the numerous waterways traveled. It also contains useful vignettes on a variety of topics, ranging from Russian architecture to souvenir shopping. Last but not least, it is full of invaluable inside tips.

Whether taking in the passing Russian countryside from a deck chair or dipping into the nightlife of St. Petersburg, you will be in the know with the book in hand. What's the story behind that interesting church on the riverbank? What kinds of fish live in this lake? Where is the most exclusive restaurant in Yaroslavl? How much should I pay for a lacquer box? Answers to all questions like these are here.

Having worked on the riverships and cruised countless times, I trust that this book will satisfy the insatiable curiosity most passengers have about the wonderland that is Russia. Presenting a mix of relevant statistics, amusing anecdotes and helpful tips, the book is sure to add an extra dimension to your adventure.

Shchastlivova puteshestviya! Bon voyage!

PREPARING FOR THE TRIP

WHY CRUISE RUSSIA?

This is the easiest question to field about Russia. You cruise Russia because no other way of touring the country comes remotely close to providing the depth, comprehensiveness and convenience of overall travel experience.

Touring Russia by river is smart. The experience comes complete with a floating hotel as a base from which to see historic parts of Russia most Russians only dream of seeing. You unpack only once, and all meals and special needs are taken care of. While onboard you are given the chance to attend language lessons, history lessons and educational lectures. You are privy to talks on Russian cuisine, instruction on native dance and tastings of traditional delicacies. You are surrounded by a native Russian staff eager to help you as well as by fellow travelers whose enthusiasm for the voyage adds to your own.

The only possible criticism of the cruise experience is that it relies on group tours and occasional bus tours—and that's no criticism at all if you enjoy group tours. To some, being herded around in a group makes for an insulated travel experience. But you are almost always free to leave the group and venture off on your own (and this book helps you do just that!). Besides, group tours in Russia may not be as shallow as you think. You receive comprehensive, detailed tours in English of the major points of interest in the historic region covered by the river route. Moreover, many museums, churches and other sights stay open just for you because your ship has reserved ground tours in advance and pays for the onshore service.

Cruising Russia by no means constitutes travel with a silver spoon, although these days it is quite comfortable. It is a voyage that will rate among your top travel adventures, with plenty of mysteries to unravel. It will give you not just a taste of Russia but the big picture, and it will do so in only two weeks and with time to spare for a deserved nap or a civilized cocktail. Now that's travel.

A RIDDLE INSIDE AN ENIGMA WRAPPED IN A MYSTERY

Let's get one thing straight: Russia is different. The urban and rural landscapes seem familiar, and the people look, more or less, like average Americans. But that appearance belies a culture, a history and a way of thinking that couldn't be more different from the culture, history and way of thinking you've encountered elsewhere. This makes Russia alternately enchanting and maddening, exciting and mystifying.

I once served as a guide for a couple from California who had come to spend a few days in St. Petersburg. While formulating our itinerary after their evening arrival, they told me they wanted to glimpse real Russian life by going to a local breakfast house the following morning. Their hearts were in the right place, but their minds were still in the West. You see, there are no breakfast houses in Russia, and like in most of Europe, eating breakfast is not nearly the institution it is in the United States. I politely suggested an alternative, as I couldn't bring myself to tell them that the best way to get to know real Russian life is to spend several hours conversing with Russians in the kitchen of a cramped apartment chain-smoking cigarettes and drinking bad coffee.

Bring an open heart and mind, leave all preconceptions at home, and you can't go wrong.

WHEN TO GO

Avg temp (hi/low)	May	June	July	Aug	Sep	Oct
Moscow	63/44	69/51	71/55	68/52	57/43	45/33
St. Petersburg	60/44	66/52	70/56	66/54	56/45	45/37

Although every ship has its own timetable, the river cruise season generally begins in mid-May and ends in mid-October. The most mild weather is to be encountered at the height of the season, which is late June to early August. This is consequently the most popular time for cruising, when ships are at full capacity and prices for cruise packages are at their highest.

Late June is also the time of white nights in the north, when the only true darkness in the sky occurs for a few minutes in the early morning as the sun hovers around the horizon as if not sure what to do next. This can be a magical time of year, but it can also compound your jet lag.

Cruising early or late in the season usually means harsher weather, particularly cold on the decks of the ship. But it also means fewer passengers on your ship, on other ships and in the ports of call. In Europe and Russia, school starts on September 1, and consequently the crowds of families seem to diminish dramatically overnight after this date.

In order to beat the bad weather, many ships make their September cruises from Moscow along the Volga down to the Black Sea. These cruises hit many historic Volga cities, but you do miss out on St. Petersburg.

WHAT TO EXPECT

Language

Russians are among the warmest people on earth, with an insatiable curiosity about the ways of the West (even though many of them now vacation there). Communication is key to getting to know your hosts, so here are a few words to the wise.

The good news is that, unlike the French, Russians do not expect you to know their language. The bad news is that the Russian language is exceedingly difficult to pronounce without a great deal of practice. Yes, like everywhere else, if you venture a few words or phrases in the native tongue you will endear yourself. But like everywhere else, you will endear yourself by making a fool of yourself, which of course is no reason not to try. The *River Cruise Phrasebook* (available at www.russiabyriver.com) is a unique resource that can give you a fighting chance at getting some intelligible Russian out of your mouth.

When speaking English, do not presume that your listener can understand everything you're saying. American English is chock-full of idioms and regional slang, not to mention distinct accents. Also, many Russians learn their English from the British model. If you want to be understood and have good verbal rapport, speak clearly, a little slower than at home and use a direct manner of expression. This is not to say you should talk to Russians as if they're deaf mutes; just remember that your Texas drawl and diction is barely intelligible to a New Yorker, let alone to a Russian.

The facility with English among the Russians you will be meeting breaks down as follows. On the ship, the onboard guides will be fluent; in fact, some of them may possess an extraordinary use of the lexicon. The restaurant and chambermaid staff will have a more basic ability and will know the words and phrases specific to their trade. The crew (mates, technicians, sailors) will have little or no grasp of the language. Off the ship, you will encounter better English in Moscow and Petersburg than in the provinces, where most of the time you will have to rely on innovative gesturing when dealing with locals.

Remember that everyone in the world now wants to learn English, and Russians are no exception. Most relish the chance to speak English with a native speaker but are understandably embarrassed. Your job is to put them at ease with a congenial manner and give them a free lesson with your impeccable, clear speech.

Food

Onboard dining has come a long way since cruises for Westerners first started operating in 1992, and now there is variation among the ships. Some companies offer top-notch continental-style dining on their ships at upper-end tour package prices, while others save you money by sticking to traditional menus oriented around the staples of the Russian diet.

Regardless of whether the chef is named François or Ivan, most onboard restaurants offer a choice of at least two dishes at every meal (unless a breakfast buffet is offered). A complimentary glass of wine and live chamber music is often also a feature of onboard meals.

If price is no object and dining well is a priority, by all means book yourself on a ship with a European-run kitchen. If, on the other hand, you are amenable to eating the native cuisine, just know that in Russia native cuisine comprises a heavy reliance on cabbage, potatoes, cucumbers, tomatoes and beets. Beef, pork and chicken feature in many dishes, while for fish, the local mainstay is pike-perch. Either way you go, rest assured that you will be fed often and fed well.

In Moscow and Petersburg it is easy to break the shipboard regime and find a nice restaurant, especially if you turn to any of the major hotels. For tips on dining ashore at any of the stops along the navigation, consult "The Inside Scoop" sections at the end of each port-of-call chapter in this book.

Accommodations
Almost all tourist cabins are located on one of the upper decks and have a large window that can be opened. Most cabins are double occupancy (a few singles and quads are available), with two berths and an ensuite bathroom. The small bathroom appears to be missing a shower, but the sink's faucet, on a hose, is pulled out and placed in a bracket on the wall for showering. Cabins also feature book shelves, cabinets, a closet, and on some ships, even a small refrigerator.

Because these are riverships, quarters are tighter than on an ocean liner, regardless of the cabin category you choose. The only cabin category that garners you a significant increase in space is the suite, of which there are precious few per ship. Suites feature a living room area with a sofa and a coffee table, and an adjoining bedroom with a queen-size bed and a roomy ensuite bathroom. If you know you will require a suite, book your cruise as early as possible and be prepared to pay two to three times the standard cabin price.

A few cruise companies have fully renovated the interiors of some of their ships, building two cabins in the space formerly used by three cabins. Accordingly, these cabins shun the old two-berth format and offer a queen bed, a desk, a television and an ensuite bathroom with freestanding shower and/or separate bathtub. If space is a major issue for you, and you are willing to pay for it, seek out one of these ships.

One generally does not spend a lot of time in the cabin, as it is always more exciting to be out on the decks or in one of the public areas. The sun deck at the rear of the ship is the perennial favorite because it provides a wonderful vantage point, lots of space and shelter from the wind. Other public areas where you are likely to spend time include the small bar at the front of the ship and the large bar at the back, the fore library and the side decks.

WHAT TO BRING

Clothing and accessories

Although Moscow, St. Petersburg and the region in between are as likely as anywhere else to experience an unexpected summertime heat wave (during which temperatures may soar into the nineties), summers are usually mild. Casual summer wear is appropriate both on and off the ship, and on nice days the wind-sheltered sun deck will be littered with sun worshipping bodies in lounge chairs.

However, being on a moving vessel on the water makes the air quite cool. In the evenings a sweater or medium-weight jacket is usually necessary to stroll comfortably around the decks. To sit in the bow of the ship, a jacket is almost always necessary. Those cruising in May or September, or anyone with cold blood, should bring a heavy jacket. Rain is frequent at all times of the summer.

The following is a list of items you should not forget.

- 1-2 nice outfits (coat and tie for men; dress or smart slacks for women) for the two dressy occasions onboard as well as for any visits to the ballet or opera in Moscow or St. Petersburg
- 1-2 sweaters and a medium-weight jacket
- For ladies, a shawl (for warmth as well as to cover your head when visiting an Orthodox service)
- Heavy jacket or light parka (for May and September cruises)
- Sunbathing gear and sandals for hot afternoons on the sun deck (may not apply to May and September cruises)
- Comfortable walking shoes
- Binoculars
- Mosquito repellent
- An umbrella and/or raincoat

- A two-week supply of any personal items or medications on which you rely daily
- Room deodorizer or your favorite home fragrance or sachet for your cabin and bathroom
- The *River Cruise Phrasebook* and other cruise essentials available at www.russiabyriver.com

Money

You actually need not take much money on a Russian river cruise, as your lodgings, transfers and meals are all paid for in advance. Here is a list of things for which you will need extra money.

• **Onboard tips.** Tips for the staff and crew are made all at once at the end of the cruise and may total as much as $100, including any personal tips.

• **Onshore tips.** It is customary to tip your local onshore guide a few dollars (or ruble equivalent) if you enjoyed the tour; should you ever take a taxi, you need not tip the driver; should you ever dine in a restaurant off the ship, a 10% tip for your waiter is adequate for excellent service.

• **Onshore food.** Have enough rubles on you to buy typical street vendor fare such as hot dogs, ice cream, beer, soda and water. If you decide to go to a café, pub or restaurant, have enough cash to cover the bill.

• **Gifts and souvenirs.** About $100 will get you a few postcards, a small matryoshka doll set, a military watch, a fur hat and a bottle of vodka. Those looking for more than this or higher quality items such as collectible hand-painted lacquer boxes, hand-crafted chess sets, coffee table books, genuine antiques, cameras, jewelry or clothing should plan on spending more.

Most ships these days operate on a credit system for extra onboard expenses, such as drinks at the bar, wine in the restaurant, laundry and optional tours. This means that you sign tabs as you go. When the ship reaches its final destination in either Petersburg or Moscow, it can connect to a banking system and run your credit card to take care of all your expenses. You are, of course, welcome to pay in cash as well.

Off the ship, all transactions by law must be conducted in rubles. Although no self-respecting souvenir vendor is going to lose a sale by refusing your American dollars, a salesperson in a proper shop or department store will simply be unable to take anything but rubles. A good rule of thumb is to carry both dollars and rubles at all times. Currency exchange offices are omnipresent, even in the provincial cities. Don't forget your passport, which, infuriatingly for everyone, is still officially required to change money in Russia.

Credit cards are increasingly being accepted throughout Russia, with many restaurants and shops accepting VISA or MasterCard. You can also get a cash advance against your credit card by visiting a major bank, although there will be a hefty commission charge. By no means, however, should you assume that a credit card alone can get you through this trip. Simply use it when you can, in order to conserve your cash. Bank machines, or ATMs, are popping up more and more, especially in Moscow and Petersburg. Do not count on them for your cash needs in Russia because it is likely that the American system does not match up with the system used by the bank in Russia. The Cirrus system is the one you want your card to work with, as it is the most popular in Europe.

When it comes to traveler's checks, some people swear by them, some people despise them. I personally have traveled around the world numerous times without ever carrying a traveler's check. If you're a devotee of traveler's checks, be aware that, even more so than in other places, you will suffer much inconvenience trying to cash them.

THE RIVER ROUTE

This portion of the book is your kilometer-by-kilometer guide to the sights along the riverbanks. You'll miss a lot while you're sleeping, dining, dancing and attending lectures, but read the whole thing anyway. It's made up of little-known stories and amusing historical commentaries, making this section alone an entertaining introduction to Russian history, geography and psychology. Please review the following instructions on its proper use.

HOW TO USE THIS SECTION:
Given that the riverships travel in two directions, utilize different itineraries and timetables, travel at varying speeds and encounter unique navigational conditions, it's tough to present a completely user-friendly account of the riverside sights. Moreover, posted distance markers are sometimes not seen for long stretches. To best deal with all these variables, this section is based on the official navigational charts used by all ships. This means several things:

(1) The guide starts from Moscow. On navigational maps, Moscow's Southern River Terminal is kilometer zero. Signposts along the shores of the route are numbered from this point.

(2) Passengers originating in St. Petersburg therefore begin reading this section backwards, from page 68. It's a bit of a hassle, but you'll get used to it.

(3) Port means left; starboard means right. Port is abbreviated "p." Starboard is abbreviated "sb." These terms direct you to the proper side of the ship from which to view a given sight. Passengers from St. Petersburg look to the opposite side of that which is indicated.

Applying the given distances can be difficult at times, but once you start using the guide from the deck, you'll quickly become accustomed to the ship's pace. Riverbank kilometer markers are posted every five kilometers but are sometimes hard to spot because of impeding conditions such as wide stretches of river, dense forests, fog or too much vodka. A pair of binoculars will help you follow the guide with utmost precision.

MOSCOW CANAL
(KM 46–165)

[KM 46] Welcome to your home away from home in Moscow, the **Moscow Northern River Terminal,** built in 1937 in "Stalinist Gothic" style to resemble a passenger ship. The red ruby star atop the 85-meter-high spire supposedly was taken from the walls of the Kremlin itself. Note the statue of polar bears on the building's north end and the statue of dolphins on the south end. Get the connection? The official kilometer zero is located not here but rather 46 kilometers and four locks farther down the Moscow Canal at the Southern River Terminal, near the Kremlin. Hence, your voyage technically begins at kilometer 46.

[KM 46–8 sb] Moscow's **Northern Cargo Port** sprawls along the bank of the **Moscow Canal** (see p. 150). Gigantic loading cranes, servicing ships from as far away as the Caspian and Baltic Seas, stand in animated postures along the port. If you spot a large concrete-and-metal warehouse, you've spied the biggest refrigerator in Moscow, where tons of fish are stored before being moved to the downtown shops to collect flies. Don't worry, the ubiquitous Moscow sushi bars bypass this place for their piscatorial inventory.

[KM 48] The **Leningrad Highway Bridge** marks the joining of the **Moscow Canal** proper to the **Khimki Reservoir,** on which the Northern River Terminal is located.

[KM 49] The **Moscow Circular Highway Bridge,** which marks the Moscow city limit, goes through the suburb of **Khimki,** which is home to sprawling suburbs and infamous Sheremetyevo Airport.

[KM 50] The ship passes under the **October Railway Bridge,** built in 1935. The clearance below the bridge sets the maximum height of canal vessels at 13.6 meters.

[KM 51–7] Verdant banks slope down both sides of the canal along this dramatic section called **Glubokaya Viyemka,** or "Deep Hollow." To establish a depth here of 23 meters, canal workers scooped out enough soil to fill a train reaching to Vladivostock. The scale of the effort is due to the fact that you're sailing through a mountain.

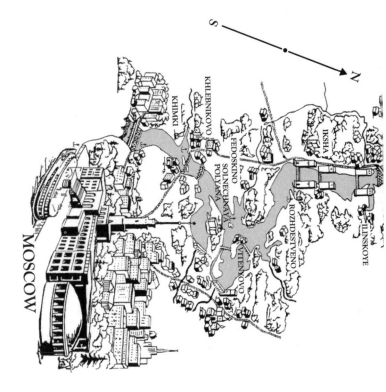

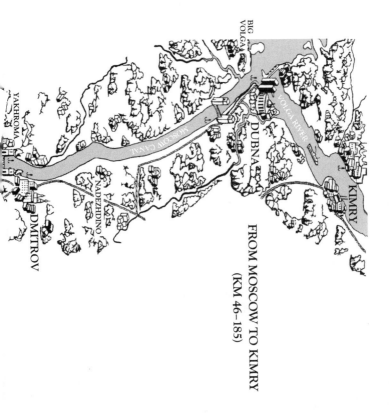

FROM MOSCOW TO KIMRY
(KM 46–185)

[KM 60 sb] A monument in the form of a small speedboat stands at the entrance to a large shipyard. This area is called the **Khlebnikovo Backwater,** formed by the mouth of the **Klyazma River,** and is home to the Moscow River Shipping Company fleet during winter. The adjacent town of **Khlebnikovo** boasts one of the region's most popular resorts, with chaize-lounges and a floating restaurant/hotel on the embankment.

[KM 61 p] The village of **Troitskoye** features a small yacht club on both sides of the canal.

[KM 66–71 sb] Next along this stretch of crooked canal you'll pass the village of **Khverevo,** situated behind a pier. Four miles inland is the village of **Zhostovo,** where they make those Russian painted trays you see in all the souvenir shops.

[KM 72 sb] An inlet here leads back to the **Uchinskoye Reservoir,** an off-limits area constituting Volga waters in the process of "settling" before being piped to the Moscow Water Station for purification. In other words, it's kind of a cesspool. On the opposite shore of the **Pyalovskoye Reservoir,** on which the ship is now sailing, a bay is formed by the mouth of the **Ucha River.** This is a popular recreation spot called **Solnechnaya Polyana,** or "Sunny Glade." More noteworthy is the village of **Fedoskino,** situated atop the riverbank but unfortunately not very visible from the ship. Fedoskino is one of the four Russian villages that produce hand-painted lacquer boxes.

[KM 74–7 sb] The settlement of **Vitenyovo** lies along this short stretch of canal between two reservoirs. Russian writer Saltykov-Shchedrin kept a mansion here. It was flooded when the reservoir was filled.

[KM 77–82] This 11.5-square-kilometer basin is called the **Pestovskoye Reservoir,** on which you'll see a number of islands. Before this area was flooded, the islands were hilltops. Passenger ships heading to Moscow often tie up at the pier in front of **Pine Grove** (*Sosnoviy bor*). The reason for the stop is that ships often are too early for their strictly allocated arrival time in Moscow and thus have some time to kill. You will likely be allowed to disembark for a few hours to stroll through the lovely forest. If there happens to be a Russian ship also docked here, her passengers are probably deep in the woods already picking berries. American passengers, who think that berries grow in little cartons beneath plastic wrap, are not advised to harvest the vegetation.

[KM 82-6] Along this short stretch of canal connecting two reservoirs lie the villages of **Protasovo** and **Rozhdestveno.** The latter is identifiable by its hydrofoil moorage and a striking stone church and belfry.

[KM 86-92] Handsome two- and three-story cottages dot the banks of the **Ikshinskoye Reservoir,** on which the ship sails. The dwellings are part of the village of **Bolshoye Ivanovskoye,** which has charge of the nice farmland.

[KM 93] Some sources refer to the sculpted figures atop the lower towers of **Lock #6** as Soviet workers, while others identify them as canal builders. Either way, it's a good example of the irony of Soviet realism, as Soviet workers tended to look downcast and dour rather than chiseled and heroic, and canal builders were political prisoners dropping like flies from starvation. The lock measures 290 x 30 x 15.5 meters, and the net change in water level is eight meters. St. Petersburg-bound ships drop; Moscow-bound ships rise. Depending on your direction, this is either the first or last lesson of your Russian locking odyssey.

[KM 93-6 p] The settlement of **Iksha** lies behind the highway and railroad that run parallel to the canal between the fifth and sixth locks.

[KM 96] In front of the upper towers of **Lock #5** stands a statue of a young woman holding aloft a model of a sailboat. Look familiar? That's because you probably saw her (well, an enlarged version of her) back at the main entrance to the Northern River Terminal in Moscow. This lock was built with some flashy architectural styles. Notice the enclosed galleries in the upper towers and the small colonnaded belvederes atop the lower towers. Around the lower part of the lock a granite staircase is decorated with urns and iron grill-work. According to official information, all these elements were incorporated to foster the lock's "harmony with the surrounding greenness of the Iksha River Valley." The lock measures 290 x 30 x 15.5 meters. The net change in water level is eight meters. St. Petersburg-bound ships drop; Moscow-bound ships rise.

[KM 103] Situated in a picturesque valley, **Lock #4,** designed to look like a triumphal arch, sports glass-enclosed observation decks in its towers (although they're not as spiffy as they sound). The lock's dimensions are 290 x 30 x 15.5 meters. The net change in water level is eight meters. St. Petersburg-bound ships drop; Moscow-bound ships rise.

[KM 104 sb] On the southern side of the **Savelovskiy Railway Bridge,** the **Yakhroma Reservoir** recedes back to the village of **Ilinskoye.**

[KM 106 p] The **Yakhroma River** is grafted onto the canal.

[KM 107] Not to be outdone, **Lock #3** has its share of anomalous adornment. The lower towers are crowned with beautiful copper replicas of none other than Christopher Columbus's famous galleon, the *Santa Maria.* If you look closely at the upper towers, you'll see bleached marks where shiny hammer-and-sickle emblems used to hang. Think of the whole thing as a visual oxymoron. The lock measures 290 x 30 x 15.5 meters. The net change in water level is eight meters. St. Petersburg-bound ships drop; Moscow-bound ships rise.

[KM 108 p] The city of **Yakhroma** grew out of a 19th century settlement which operated one of the region's first textile plants. At last check, the factory was still functioning. The **Yakhroma Bridge**, which connects the factory to the city, was the setting of its share of WWII drama, as evidenced by the bronze statue of a soldier at the bridge's eastern approach.

[KM 108-15 p] The **Yakhroma River** flows parallel to the canal.

[KM 115 sb] The church standing behind all the cranes in the port of **Dmitrov** is the Assumption Cathedral, built in the 16th century. Its architecture is reminiscent of that of the Archangel Michael Cathedral in the Moscow Kremlin. But that's not all Dmitrov has in common with the capital. The two cities were founded by the same prince, Yury Dolgoruky (the Long-Armed), who first came here on a tax-collecting mission in 1154. Dolgoruky was traveling with a princess, who according to history, "along the way gave birth to a son, Dmitry." So the prince founded a fortress called Dmitrov, which eventually grew into a city. The city itself was one of Russia's largest and most populated in the 15th and 16th centuries, but later underwent a long period of decline.

In the 1920s it was a quiet little town of 5,000 inhabitants. In the 1930s it became Moscow Canal construction headquarters and exploded into a demi-metropolis of 60,000 people.

[KM 127–30 sb] The village of **Nadezhdino** (derived from *nadezhda*, meaning "hope") lies at the north end of this long, narrow bend in the canal. Navigators are busy communicating with each other here to avoid collisions. You hope.

[KM 151] The banks beside **Lock #2** feature their share of impressive landscaping. You might see some flower beds, fountains and decorative lattice. More likely, you'll see local kids on bikes prodding you to throw them some candy, gum or better yet, cash. As to the figures on the lock towers, on the left you have three rank-and-file Soviet workers; on the right the threesome is comprised of a pilot, a soldier and a border guard. Why? Why not. The lock itself measures 290 x 30 x 13.5 meters. The net change in water level here is six meters. St. Petersburg-bound ships drop; Moscow-bound ships rise.

[KM 160] The **Sestra River,** or "Sister River," crosses the canal. Note that the river has been artificially diverted beneath the canal.

[KM 162 sb] As the ship turns near the lock, you'll see the **Big Volga** lighthouse.

[KM 164 p] On the shore amidst the trees stands **Lenin.** Many ships pass him in the dead of night, so in case you miss him, here is my brother's impression: "A very granite father of socialism is striking an observant, grandfatherly pose, his gaze on Mother Volga. One hand rests behind his back, as if concealing something, the other is outstretched, as if it should be holding a snifter of cognac. Flowers rise up from the base of the statue, while from the head, bird excrement trickles down. If you look back after passing the figure, it appears as if Lenin has three legs."

[KM 165] The **Volga River** (see p. 152) is joined to the **Moscow Canal** by **Lock #1** of the Moscow Canal. The dimensions of the chamber are 290 x 30 x 18.5 m. The net change in water level here is 11 meters. St. Petersburg-bound ships drop; Moscow-bound ships rise.

VOLGA RIVER
(KM 166–385)

[KM 166–73 sb] The city of **Dubna** actually is situated on an island surrounded by the Dubna and Sestra Rivers, the Volga River and the Moscow Canal. Dubna is dubbed the "capital of the peaceful atom" owing to its Institute for Nuclear Research, where scientists and physicists from around the world come to work on, er, peaceful nuclear issues. Before reaching the institute, you will pass a long stretch of drab Soviet high-rises facing grand, "new Russian" dachas under construction across the river. Then come an indoor swimming pool, a patch of pleasant beach and a colorful boatyard. Well before reaching Dubna you might notice a big sign on the shore reading "Dubna" (ДУБНА). This sign demarcates the region of Dubna rather than the city proper.

[KM 174 sb] On the northern outskirts of Dubna, where the mouth of the **Dubna River** joins the Volga, are a church and a horse ranch.

[KM 175–6 p] Occasionally a local villager, a white-bearded fellow with a peculiar zeal for life, can be seen on the shore greeting the dawn in a naked salute.

[KM 185] Ships heading for Moscow are required to stop for a sanitary inspection at the city of **Kimry.** According to regulations designed to safeguard the water of the Moscow Canal, inspectors board the ships to seal the dark water tanks. Usually ships purify their own dark water and expel it along the way. The water of the Moscow Canal, devoid of much current, is rather fragile, so as a precaution ships have to "hold it in" until they reach a purification plant in Moscow.

Sanitation issues aside, Kimry itself boasts a colorful history. Kimry in the 17th century became a center of shoe production. Why? Because a popular cattle route ran right by the city. Shoes and boots became Kimry's bread and butter for the next three hundred years. Local literature claims that Kimry shoes used to be as famous as Tula samovars, Vologda lace and Ivanovo linen. And who would dispute that? After all, Kimry boots were worn by Peter the Great's soldiers, and according to a local booklet, it was "in Kimry boots that the Soviet Army reached Berlin."

In the 19th century, when over 15,000 shoemakers inhabited the city, it hosted a semi-annual footwear trade fair. Kimry shoemakers constituted an elite peasant class who took pride in their dress and decorum. They also enjoyed imbibing large quantities of vodka, perhaps giving birth to the Russian expression "drunk as a cobbler." During Soviet times, all of the private shoe brands were "united" under the label Red Star, the Soviet answer to Converse. As you pass by, you will be able to see the city's coat of arms, which is painted on the riverside cement dyke. Yes, that is a sailship with a depiction of a boot on the sail.

[KM 187–8 p] The quaint Two Captains' Yacht Club can be seen across the river from a large shipyard. A free copy of the *Russia by River Photo Album* will go to anyone who can send us information about these mysterious two captains.

[KM 200 sb] An aged church, flanked by monstrous power lines, stands near the village of **Beloye**.

[KM 205 sb] Directly across from the 205 kilometer marker stands the white stone St. George Church. It's probable that at one time most of the buildings around here were made of white stone, as this is **Beliy Gorodok,** or "White Town," settled in the 14th century. Today the town is engaged in ship repairing and plays wintertime host to much of the Moscow Shipping Company fleet.

[KM 219 p] The village of **Medveditskoye** lies at the mouth of the **Medveditsa River,** where there once stood a mighty fortress, now in ruins. This was a popular place for fortifications, as the river for centuries served as border between the Tver and Novgorod principalities.

[KM 231 sb] The village of **Sknyatino,** situated at the mouth of the **Nerl River,** was founded by Yury Dolgoruky, the same long-armed prince who founded Moscow. Ever since its first mention in the Chronicles in 1134, Sknyatino was considered a lovely city, so much so that the princes of the Kiev and Vladimir-Suzdal principalities constantly fought over it. By fighting for it, naturally, they destroyed it. During the next century it was rebuilt, but then Mongol-Tatars came and burned it to the ground. It seems never to have recovered.

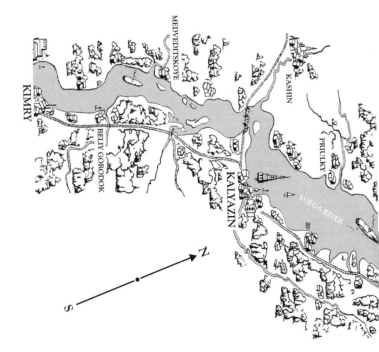

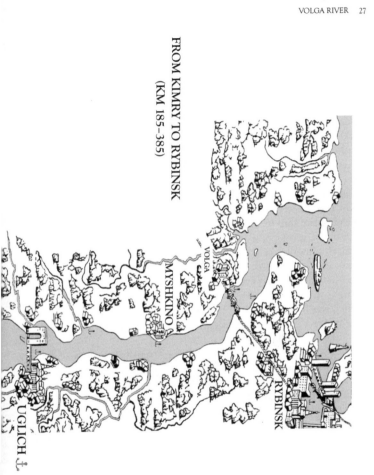

FROM KIMRY TO RYBINSK
(KM 185–385)

UGLICH

MYSHKINO

VOLGA

RYBINSK

[KM 238 sb] Some ships make their "green stop" here on the shores of **Novookatovo.** A smattering of dachas, a park, a pier and a sanatorium lie along the banks.

[KM 244 sb] You might be able to catch a glimpse of a bust of Pushkin to the left of a small white chapel in the village of **Nikitskoye.** With all that splendid writing, he occasionally needed to take the mineral waters at nearby Kashin, and he stayed here from time to time.

[KM 249 p] The mouth of the **Kashinka River** opens on the north side of the **Kashinskiy Bridge** in the city of **Kashin.** On this bridge the St. Petersburg–Moscow railroad crosses the Volga. The city itself was founded in 1238 and is known for its sulphur-rich mineral springs, the water from which allegedly treats intestinal disorders, rheumatism and other maladies.

[KM 260 sb] As the river bends, an enormous satellite dish can be seen ahead of the ship in the distance. This means it is time to get ready for one of the most popular onboard photo opportunities of the navigation, the **flooded belfry of Kalyazin.** Erected in 1800 as part of the St. Nicholas Cathedral on Kalyazin's Market Square, the belfry formerly stood 70 meters high and was considered among the finest structures along the Volga. You are now sailing over Kalyazin's Market Square, which was flooded to dam the river at the Uglich Hydroplant. The upper portion of the belfry, recently planted on an unattractive earthen foundation, is all that survives.

[KM 280 p] At the mouth of the **Puksha River** sits the village of **Priulky,** with a dilapidated church and a severed belfry.

[KM 280-98] This stretch of Volga is recognizable by its west bank rising high above the water in sharp precipices and its thickly forested, lower east bank.

[KM 298-302 p] Along this crooked stretch of river lie the villages of **Kotovo** and **Korozhechno** as well as a couple of churches, one of which is in derelict condition.

[KM 310] Entering the lock of the **Uglich Hydroplant,** ships pass through a triumphal arch, built to commemorate victory over Germany. The facility, completed in 1940, is operated by only two personnel. The lock itself measures 290 x 30 x 18.5 meters. The net change in water level here is 11 meters. St. Petersburg-bound ships drop; Moscow-bound ships rise.

[KM 312] The ship ties up beneath the high embankment of the ancient city of **Uglich** (see p. 89). To the right, in the old kremlin, the splendid Church of St. Dmitry on the Blood with its star-studded cupolas and the green-domed Transfiguration Cathedral await your inspection.

[KM 313 sb] Adjacent to Uglich, in the village of **Zolotoruchye,** a smart multi-domed church complements those of the Uglich embankment.

[KM 315 p] Only a few kilometers from Uglich, the Volga bends ninety degrees at the mouth of the **Korozhechna River.**

[KM 320 p] The village of **Voskresenskaya,** or "Resurrection," features a church of the same name.

[KM 344 p] Several ships call here at ancient **Myshkino.** The legend of its founding begins when one day a local feudal lord grew weary while hunting and fell asleep. He was awakened by a mouse scampering over his face. He then noticed that a snake was poised to attack him. He killed the snake and ordered a chapel built on the spot where the mouse had saved his life. The settlement that grew alongside the church was called Myshkino, meaning "Mouse's" village. Myshkino grew into a lively mercantile center with multi-colored stone streets lined with some of the Volga's finest mansions and cathedrals. The Bolshevik Revolution put an end to all that, but today the town is rebounding slowly thanks in part to the ships that stop here bringing foreign tourists to tour the museum of wooden architecture and the one-of-a-kind Museum of Mice, housed in the residence of a wealthy Myshkino merchant of yesteryear.

[KM 347 sb] A modest church stands in the small village of **Okhotino.**

[KM 363 sb] The ship passes a town named—no kidding—Town (*Gorodok*).

[KM 367 p] A railway bridge spans the river at the village of **Volga.** A few pillars might be sticking out of the water around here; they're remnants of an older bridge.

[KM 372 sb] An old brick church stands in the village of **Ivanovskoye.**

[KM 385 sb] The village of **Koprino** marks the division between the **Rybinsk Reservoir** and the **Volga River.**

DOWN THE VOLGA
TO YAROSLAVL AND KOSTROMA

NOTE ON KILOMETER COUNT: Because this segment of the journey is a side trip of sorts, kilometers are counted separately. To maintain consistency with the actual navigational charts used by riverships, this section commences tallying Volga kilometers from an invisible reference point called the Bermuda Triangle in the south of the Rybinsk Reservoir. The Bermuda Triangle is located 410 kilometers from Moscow. Thus the trip down the Volga begins at **KM 410,** here referred to as **VOLGA 410.** The net addition of the Volga roundtrip to your overall total is 380 kilometers.

[VOLGA 410] Actually located in the Rybinsk Reservoir, this is the southeastern tip of the **Bermuda Triangle,** an invisible navigational reference point from which the voyage down the Volga technically starts.

[VOLGA 422 sb] At the approach to the Rybinsk Hydroplant, **Mother Volga** extends a welcoming hand. In her other hand she holds the draft plan for harnessing the Volga's waters for electricity. A famous Lenin quotation about the electrification of the country used to be inscribed on the base of the monument. Ships passing Mother Volga late at night sometimes illuminate her with their spotlights, allowing passengers to wonder about that giant petrel flying around Mother Volga's shins.

[VOLGA 423] The ship glides beneath a pedestrian overpass at the approach to the **Rybinsk Hydroplant.** Technically, the hydroplant is located in two rivers, neither of which is here anymore. The dam and hydrostation lie in the old mouth of the Sheksna River, and the lock, in the former bed of the Volga. The entire hydroplant wasn't officially completed until 1950, although during WWII it almost single-handedly supplied Moscow with electricity. (Its snow-filled, unfinished appearance spared it from Luftwaffe attacks.) The hydroplant consists of two separate and parallel locks, the fastest filling of the journey, **Lock #11** and **Lock #12.** Each measures 290 x 30 x 21 meters. Ships heading down the Volga drop 14 meters, the greatest water level change of the journey.

[VOLGA 424] Exiting the lock, ships navigate the waters of the **Volga River** (see p. 152). Once past the upcoming city of Rybinsk, the stretch of river all the way to Kostroma is known to navigators as the "tea party" of the journey. Why? Because it's such a wide and deep stretch of river that they can sit back, relax and have tea. Or vodka.

[VOLGA 425–40] With a population of around 300,000, the city of **Rybinsk** stretches along both banks of the Volga. No stranger to Russian naming games, the city's name was changed to Shcherbakov (a Party notable) in 1946, then to Andropov after the former general secretary's death in 1984. During *perestroika*, it once again became Rybinsk ("Fish Town"), the name most closely associated with the settlement's origins as a 12th century Slavic fishing center. Rybinsk officially became a city in 1777, after Peter the Great's Mariinskaya Canal System had made the settlement an important trading port. Wheat was the major trade here; even today ships laden with wheat can be seen in the port.

An unmistakable sight in Rybinsk is the neoclassical, five-domed Savior-Transfiguration Cathedral with its towering baroque belfry, gilded spire and recently refurbished glittering cupolas. Built in the mid-19th century, the cathedral could have ended up in St. Petersburg's St. Isaac's Square but that its plan was rejected in favor of that of the present St. Isaac's Cathedral. Other prominent structures along Rybinsk's right bank include the colonnaded, blue and white river terminal, built in 1811; the New Bread Exchange, an immaculately restored, 20th century, German-style tiled palace perched at the river front; and a 28-meter-high obelisk commemorating local WWII heroes.

[VOLGA 448 p] Through a gap in the trees, after a red-brick belfry, you should be able to glimpse a dilapidated, white 18th century mansion called **Tikhvinskoye,** built in 1767. A military officer and aspiring aristocrat named Tushinin built the mansion in order to repose in its library with a glass of brandy and a good novel and feel like a man of taste and distinction—and to invite guests over to witness him being a man of taste and distinction. Upon hearing that Catherine the Great was to travel the Volga, Tushinin became obsessed with the dream of hosting the empress so that she too could behold his taste and distinction. Unfortunately, his little social coup never materialized.

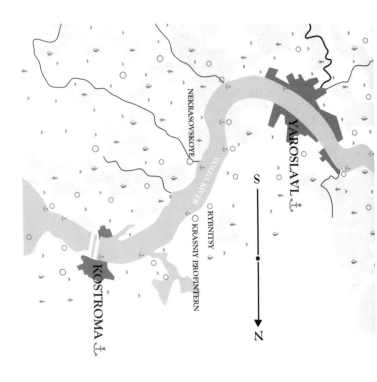

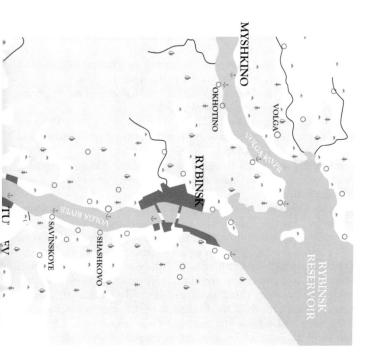

[VOLGA 449 sb] On a verdant hilltop near a pier marking the village of **Krasnoye** stand the remains of a narrow church built in 1724 in Petrine baroque style.

[VOLGA 453 sb] The town of **Pesochnoye** (derived from the Russian *pesok*, or "sand") is known for its porcelain manufactory, a sprawling complex of rundown red brick buildings and smokestacks built in 1884.

[VOLGA 455 p] The village of **Shashkovo** was home to the ancestors of that man of taste and distinction, Tushinin. A neoclassical church, built in 1775, and an early 19th century belfry stand on the bank.

[VOLGA 460 p] Amid the trees hide five brown domes of the Epiphany Church in the village of **Khopylevo.**

[VOLGA 467 p] The red-brick Church of Archangel Michael (1779), with tiny gray cupolas and a spired belfry, stands in the village of **Savinskoye,** adjacent to a grassy clearing.

[VOLGA 472 sb] In the village of **Bogoslovskoye** stands the striking Church of St. John the Divine (1882), with copper cupolas and a towering white belfry.

[VOLGA 480–3 p] The church-strewn town of **Tutaev** is named after Red Army hero Ilya Tutaev. The original name was Romanov, as the settlement was founded in 1283 by Prince Roman of Yaroslavl. It is entirely possible that by the time you pass Tutaev, it will be Romanov once again. The town flourished in the late 18th century, when it's populace comprised icon painters, silversmiths, carpenters, weavers, and shipbuilders and its many churches were erected. The particularly striking, cherry-colored Church of the Exaltation of the Cross is perched close to the water looking as if plucked from a Russian fairy tale. Up on the high bank is the Kazan Transfiguration Church, with its white belfry. You might also catch a glimpse of the modest, one-domed Intercession Church and the Savior's Archangel Church. On the opposite bank stands the 17th century Ascension Cathedral. Known for "preserving the feel of the Russian provinces," Tutaev used to be popular with artists, who came here to paint the avenues of old mansions and ornately carved wooden houses.

[VOLGA 488 sb] Inland, in the town of **Konstantinovskoye,** is the Mendeleyev Chemical Plant, named after the famous Russian scientist who developed the Periodic Table of Elements.

[VOLGA 495 sb] Before the Volga makes a gradual ninety degree bend, you can catch sight of a dilapidated, medieval-looking church outside the village of **Petropolovskoye.**

[VOLGA 502 p] The **It River** empties into the Volga; an old belfry marks the spot.

[VOLGA 506 sb] The 13th century town of **Norskoye,** with several visible churches, lies on the bank.

[VOLGA 512 p] The nearly 700-year-old **Tolga Monastery** stands amidst groves of cedar at the water's edge. The monastery walls, whose towers are crowned by gray spires, enclose two main churches. The Savior's Cathedral is topped by a dozen domes surrounding a singularly elevated cupola. The white stone Cathedral of the Introduction to the Temple, with five large green cupolas, is flanked by a chapel and an elegant belfry with a tiny cupola. Hanging in the belfry is the largest bell ever cast by craftsman Fyodor Motorin, whose son went on to cast the gigantic Tsar Bell in the Moscow Kremlin.

According to legend, the monastery was founded in 1314 when its first church was built as a tribute to a miracle that occurred on the spot. Bishop Trifon of Yaroslavl, while camping at the mouth of the Tolga River, was awakened by a pillar of fire on the opposite shore. A footbridge then extended to him. He crossed the bridge to find a flaming icon of the Virgin. Like a good bishop, he dropped to his knees and prayed heartily. When he returned to camp, he discovered that his belongings were missing. His traveling companions boated across the river and found both the icon and the bishop's things. When word of the event spread, believers built a church here to house the icon.

The monastery was closed by the Bolsheviks in 1926 and subsequently turned into a "labor education colony." In 1988 the monastery was given back to the Orthodox Church, which restored it and turned it into the Tolga Convent.

[VOLGA 516-22] The sheer, manicured embankment crowned by colonnaded gazebos belongs to one of the oldest cities on the Volga, **Yaroslavl** (see p. 97), where ships drop anchor for the day.

[VOLGA 525 sb] While cruising through the industrial outskirts of Yaroslavl, you'll notice a factory bearing a huge slogan reading: "Don't pollute the Volga!" Yet the Volga is visibly at its filthiest around here, an irony apparently lost on all the fishermen floating in bands of rafts.

[VOLGA 533-60] Along this picturesque stretch of river several small villages and churches are set amidst birch, alder and cherry trees.

[VOLGA 564-9 p] A dam protects the bank from flooding below the village of **Rybnitsy.** In 1841 one Alexander Opekushin was born into serfdom here. He eventually saved enough rubles to buy his freedom and developed his talents as a sculptor. His work became noticed by the right people, and soon he was commissioned to create several prominent statues. Pieces of his that you can see during your trip include the statue of Peter the Great in Petrozavodsk, the Pushkin statue in Moscow's Pushkin Square and the supporting figures in the monument to Catherine the Great along St. Petersburg's Nevsky Prospekt.

[VOLGA 571 p] In the town of **Krasniy Profintern** stands a 150-year-old plant which processes starch and syrup.

[VOLGA 597-604] The golden domes sparkling above fortress walls at the mouth of the **Kostroma River** belong to the Ipatievsky Monastery, one of the country's most famous, situated in the town of **Kostroma** (see p. 105). Once docked at the river terminal, you may not see the "white city on seven hills wearing a necklace of green gardens" described by local literature, but you will be visiting a town still adored as the quintessence of provincial Russia.

[VOLGA 660] In 1995 one or two ships began calling on historic **Plyos.** It is a charming town of only 3,500 inhabitants, picturesque at every step. If it catches on as a major stop, you can be sure to read more about it in subsequent editions of *Russia by River*.

RYBINSK RESERVOIR
(KM 385–528)

[KM 385–528] The ship traverses the **Rybinsk Reservoir** (see p. 154) along a north-south axis. Sometimes called the Rybinsk Sea because of its large size, in actuality this is a massive flood basin covering the natural beds of many different rivers, including the Volga and Sheksna. The flooding of the basin in 1941 was largely kept under wraps because of the mass destruction, human displacement and ecological damage it necessitated. There is not much to point out sightwise, except for what you are sailing *over*. For example, at the southern end, where a large church and belfry stand on the western shore, the ship cruises over the point where the Volga used to meet the Mologa River at the ancient city of Mologa. Founded back in the 12th century, Mologa was a colorful regional center known ever since the 16th century for its lively annual trade fair. At the time of its flooding, it was a declining town of stone and wooden dwellings, many churches, a monastery and a population of 7,000 people.

Mologa also marks a significant navigational point called the **Bermuda Triangle** by chartmen. It's named such not because ships disappear here, but rather because a few kilometers are lost at the intersection of three navigational paths. It's rather complicated, so don't worry about it.

ALONG THE VOLGA-BALTIC CANAL:
SHEKSNA RIVER AND RESERVOIR
(KM 528–714)

[KM 528] The **Sheksna River** (see p. 157) empties into the **Rybinsk Reservoir.** Navigation buffs might be interested to note that from here to St. Petersburg white and red navigational buoys are employed, while from here to Moscow black and red buoys are used. If you don't know which color designates left and which designates right then you don't care about all this anyway.

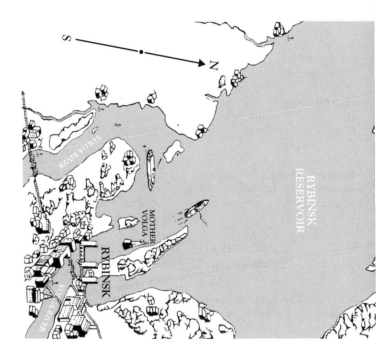

ACROSS THE RYBINSK SEA
(KM 385–533)

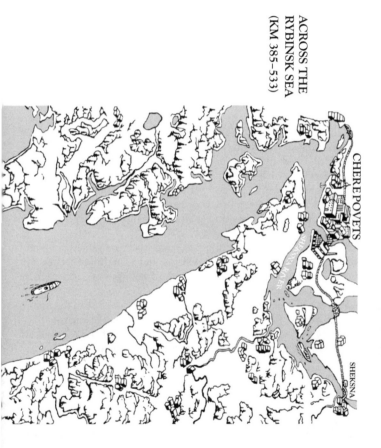

CHEREPOVETS

SHEKSNA

[KM 533–43] About the city of **Cherepovets** a Soviet guidebook offers, "The abundance of loading cranes and the crowd of cargo ships along the port speak eloquently for the successful enterprises of the city." In translation it means that this city of 300,000 people is a sprawling industrial setting, a declared environmental disaster area, and one profoundly ugly place. They've been building ships here since 1861, today concentrating on tugboats and barges. The main industry, however, is metallurgy, initiated here after WWII. More than 100 different metals are extracted and forged beneath those mighty smokestacks. According to local literature, the city's second biggest industrial enterprise is a chemical plant "which uses the by-products of the metal plant." Maybe that explains the gray soot covering all the shrubs and buildings downtown.

[KM 535] The ship sails under the **October Bridge,** a unique center-suspension construction spanning over a kilometer, weighing more than 7,000 tons and tower 85 meters over the water. It is the only one of its kind you will see on the journey—or perhaps ever.

[KM 549 sb] You might see timber awaiting transport on a pier in front of the village of **Lapach**.

[KM 552–68] Along this twisting stretch of river you can see an island or two, a few wooden piers, several villages, and a handful of dachas. You might notice metal roofing on many of the dwellings—it's a consequence of the proximity to Cherepovets, a metallurgical center.

[KM 569 p] The ship cruises under a railway bridge close to the mouth of the **Konoma River.** On the bank lies a smattering of dachas.

[KM 584 p] The remains of an old wooden lock of the Mariinskaya Canal System can be seen near the village of **Sudbitsy.**

[KM 591–6 sb] The city of **Sheksna** originated in 1905 as a railway junction outpost. It gained prominence with the construction of the neighboring hydroplant and today thrives on timber processing and dairy farming. The popular Vologda brand of butter is produced here. It also is a center for growing and processing flax, a substance which, according to writer Vasily Belov, occupies a distinct place in the heart of Russian women: "Flax for many hundreds of years has been a companion to woman's fate. It is their joy and grief, starting with the boys' diapers, proceeding to the young girls' shawls, and ending finally with a pall." No comment.

[KM 596] The **Sheksna Hydroplant** consists of a hydrostation, uncharacteristically built into the concrete dam, and **Locks #7 and #8.** The locks lie side by side and are both operable. Lock #8 opened in 1992 to alleviate the heavy traffic common to this hydroplant. Large passenger ships usually pass through Lock #8, which measures 310 x 21.5 x 22.8 meters. The older Lock #7 measures 265 x 17.5 x 19.7 meters. The net change in water level in both locks is 13 meters. There is a brief change in slope here, as ships heading to St. Petersburg finally rise, while Moscow-bound ships drop. Incidentally, this hydroplant marks the joining of the **Sheksna Reservoir,** with its wide floodwaters, to the **Lower Sheksna River,** with its more natural, narrow and winding course.

[KM 603-13] A succession of small villages and farm plots can be seen along both shores of this wide stretch of river.

[KM 613 p] Many ships make their "green stop" here on the shore below the village of **Irma.** Before partaking of the *shashlik* picnic prepared by your crew, you might venture back along the dirt road to the **Irdomka River** for a swim. Those more sight-oriented might seek out Irma's small church or a nearby monolith to Russian historian N.D. Chechulin, who died here in 1927. The villagers, comprising farmers and *dachniki,* are extremely friendly, and you might be invited to sample some fresh milk or beckoned into a home for a *ryumka* of vodka. Beware that many passengers have ended up pretty drunk after these friendly visits, so you might want to sample the milk before imbibing the vodka. Hanging around the newly built tourist complex with its bar, café and souvenir shop could keep you out of trouble—plus it's a good place to try Russian beer.

[KM 623 p] In the village of **Gorka** stand the remains of a church, surrounded by trees at the riverfront. On the opposite shore is the village of **Bolshoy Dvor.**

[KM 623-33 sb] Spread along the high banks of this picturesque stretch of reservoir lie too many typical Russian villages to name.

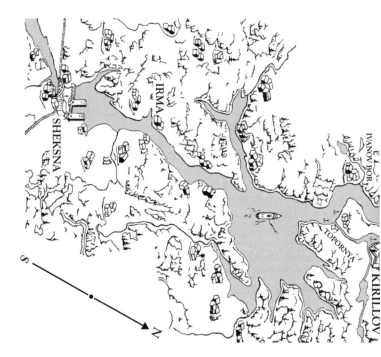

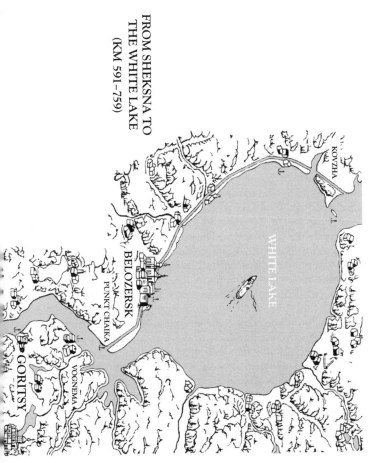

FROM SHEKSNA TO
THE WHITE LAKE
(KM 591–759)

WHITE LAKE

KOVZHA

BELOZERSK

PUNKT CHAIKA

GORITSY

VOGNEMA

[KM 635–62] Called the **Sizminskiy Floodwaters,** this massive basin resembling a lake formerly was a shallow and winding stretch of the Sheksna River. Teams of horses sometimes were required to pull barges over the shallow rapids. Tree trunks from those days can be seen protruding out of the water.

[KM 662] This point marks the border between the **Upper Sheksna River** and the **Sheksna Reservoir.** Don't look for any markers, as it's more or less an arbitrary division.

[KM 665 sb] Tucked into the reeds near large timber piles hides the first wooden lock of the **Toporninskiy Canal.** The canal is part of the 127-kilometer-long Northern Dvina System. Built in 1825-28 and reconstructed in 1916-21, this network of rivers, canals and locks was designed to open up navigation to the north from the Volga via the Sheksna. It is primarily used for local transport these days. In the 1970s the central government, looking for something to fill their five-year plan, proposed a major overhaul of the system. The plan called for channeling northern waterways (including the White Sea and Lake Onega) via the Northern Dvina River into the Sheksna and down to the Volga. The idea was to bolster the water supply in southern regions like Kazakhstan. This wacky proposal entailed not only construction of hydropower stations and mass flooding of inhabited areas, but also reversing the flow of several major waterways, including lakes as big as Onega. For once reason won out, and the project was scrapped.

[KM 667 sb] Hydrofoils frequently stop at a makeshift pier at the village of **Topornya.** There used to be a proper pier here serviced by monthly Nizhny Novgorod–St. Petersburg steamships.

[KM 669] Vast timber yards are visible on both shores.

[KM 670–2 p] Perched on a high bank, the settlement of **Ivanov Bor** ("Ivan's Grove") is a jewel to behold, with grand wooden homes, neat plots of land and tidy riverfront potato patches.

[KM 673 sb] Mounds of concrete mix lie on barges docked along the shore. The mixing goes on in the nearby green and white structures.

[KM 683] The appearance of the rustic Resurrection Convent at the river's edge signals your arrival at the village of **Goritsy** (see p. 111). Most ships lay to here while their passengers are taken by bus to tour the Monastery of St. Kyrill of the White Lake in the neighboring village of Kirillov.

[KM 687] Just outside Goritsy, the ship sails between two islands, **Gora Gorodok** and **Gora Nikitskaya.** These are names for mountains, which these islands used to be before the Sheksna was flooded.

[KM 687–96] Like many areas along the Sheksna, this is a stretch of flooded forest caused by hydroplant construction.

[KM 703 sb] In the village of **Vognema** stands a quaint church.

[KM 707 p] At **Punkt Chaika,** or "Seagull Point," stands an **obelisk** marking the entrance to the **White Lake Canal,** which enables small crafts to bypass the occasionally tumultuous White Lake.

[KM 713] The gloomy, deciduous forests on both banks and the long pontoon bridge (submerged when ships pass) attracted the eye of renowned Russian director Vasily Shukshin, who filmed the Russian classic *Krasnaya ryabina* ("*Red Rowan Tree*") here.

[KM 714 sb] Always a favorite photo-opportunity, the flooded **Church of Krokhino** stands in the mouth of the **Upper Sheksna River.** The 19th century structure, officially called the Nativity Church, is the lone symbol of an ancient past. In the 15th century Prince Gleb of Belozersk took shelter in this area during a nasty storm and ordered a church built in appreciation of the haven. A few years later he added an entire monastery, this time out of gratitude for his blind three-year-old son's miraculously gaining eyesight. The monastery stood here for more than 500 years. The village of Krokhino was founded a few centuries later and thrived as an important White Lake port. When the White Lake Canal opened in 1846, ships began bypassing Krokhino. The city entered into decline, and the monastery suffered neglect. The Soviets finally obliterated the place in the 1960s, flooding it to facilitate the construction of the Sheksna hydroplants.

ALONG THE VOLGA-BALTIC CANAL:
WHITE LAKE
(KM 714-59)

[KM 714-59] Traversing the **White Lake** (see p. 158) takes only about two hours. Although this naturally formed lake is quite large (1,380 square kilometers), it is still technically considered part of the Volga-Baltic Canal. There is not much to point out here, as ships tend to cut directly across the middle of the lake. You may be able to see the ancient city of **Belozersk,** situated on the southern shore. Ever since the eighth century there have been settlements in the Belozersk region. Present-day Belozersk is about ten kilometers from the original city of Beloozero, which was wiped out by bubonic plague in the 14th century. With binoculars you should be able to pick out a couple of churches. They are likely the Assumption Church, built by the order of Ivan the Terrible in 1553, and the Transfiguration Cathedral, built a little later by order of Ivan's son, Tsar Fyodor. During the 19th century Belozersk was one of Russia's main lace-weaving centers. Today the city, with over 50 architectural monuments, serves as home port to numerous ships and hydrofoils and is a timber and fish distribution center.

ALONG THE VOLGA-BALTIC CANAL:
KOVZHA RIVER & WATER DIVISION CANAL
(KM 759-855)

[KM 759] The **White Lake** and the **Kovzha River** (see p. 158) meet at the Kovzha's swollen estuary.

[KM 761 sb] A 200-year-old friend to navigators, the stone Purification Church can be seen on a small island. The island was a small hill in the old village of **Kovzha,** where the St. Nicholas Monastery once stood. Along with 220 other villages, Kovzha was flooded as part of the upriver canal construction. Of the mass displacement that resulted, one Soviet guidebook offers in a chit-chatty way: "It was taken by the [tens of thousands of] people as a personal tragedy."

[KM 765 p] At the north end of the White Lake another white **obelisk** protrudes out of the water, marking the other end of the narrow **White Lake Canal**.

[KM 772 sb] The Kovzha spills over into the forest at the mouths of the **Kema** and **Sholopast Rivers.** Flooding along the opposite bank is caused by the mouth of the **Shola River.**

[KM 772–6] Navigators will be on the lookout for floating wood in this flooded forest area.

[KM 781 p] At a bend in the river one of the Kovzha's tributaries, the **Kitla River,** opens its 600-meter-wide mouth.

[KM 781–91] This stretch of river is welcomed by navigators, as it was recently widened and deepened. It is also a picturesque area with forested banks and numerous small tributaries (whose names are too tongue-twisting to mention) feeding the Kovzha.

[KM 791 p] On the shore of a small bay, at the mouth of the **Solonka River,** lies a group of wooden houses adjacent to a lumberyard. This is the village of **Kurdyug,** marked by a sign on a wooden dock. Kurdyug was formerly a penal colony specializing in wood-chopping.

[KM 802 p] On the shore in a vast clearing stands a landmark well known to navigators. Called the "lonely tree," it is, well, a lonely tree. At last sighting, though, it was being kept company by an old broken-down bus. This is a rather shallow and rocky segment of canal called **Konstantinovskiye Porogi,** or "Konstantin's Rapids." This area is significant because here the canal joins the old Kovzha riverbed, thus marking the beginning or the end (depending on your direction) of the elusive **Kovzha River.**

[KM 818 p] A decrepit yet elegant wooden church hides behind the trees.

[KM 823 sb] A vast riverside lumberyard sports all the tools of the trade—mills, cranes, barges and astoundingly large piles of timber.

[KM 824] The rather desolate albeit ancient settlement of **Annenskiy Most** is sprinkled on both sides of the river. It's a timber transport center, so you'll likely see rafts and barges to the left of the small river terminal.

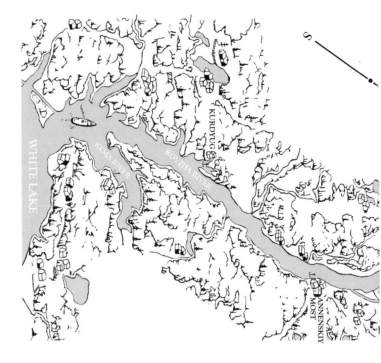

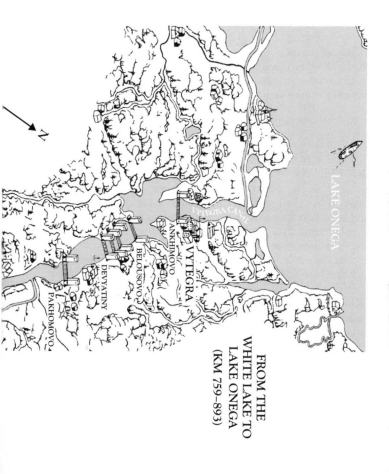

N

LAKE ONEGA

VYTEGRA CANAL

ANKHIMOVO

VYTEGRA

BELOUSOVO

DEVYATINY

PAKHOMOVO

FROM THE
WHITE LAKE TO
LAKE ONEGA
(KM 759–893)

The two sides of town are connected by a rope-drawn ferry-raft, which you won't see, as it will be submerged to allow the ship to pass.

[KM 838 p] The village of **Rubezh,** meaning "Border," is named such because it lies on the watershed of the Baltic and Volga water basins. Elevation here is 118.5 meters. During the early 1800s a hospital for laborers working on the Mariinskaya System was here. Scurvy was the malady of the day.

[KM 838–855] The ship glides along a narrow stretch of canal (50-100 meters across) on which the speed limit is 12 kilometers per hour to prevent further riverbank erosion.

ALONG THE VOLGA-BALTIC CANAL: VYTEGRA CANAL AND RESERVOIRS
(KM 855-93)

[KM 855] Lock #6 at the **Pakhomovskiy Hydroplant** is the first or last lock (depending on your direction) of the Volga–Baltic Canal's northern slope. When the lock is full, the ship is 80 meters above Lake Onega and 116 meters above St. Petersburg. The net change in water level here is 16.25 meters. St. Petersburg-bound ships drop; Moscow-bound ships rise. The dimensions of the lock are 264 x 17.7 x 23.5 meters. Locking enthusiasts might be interested to know that the lock chambers along this canal are filled and drained through gills at the upper gate rather than through underwater galleries.

[KM 855–61 sb] Between Locks #6 and #5 the ship cruises the **Novinkinskoye Reservoir.** The main settlement here is the ancient village of **Devyatiny.** Its five-domed, wooden Assumption Church, built in 1770, offers a fine example of the striking northern architecture featured most prominently on Kizhi Island. While the Mariinskaya System was in use, the folks of Devyatiny made a living by transporting ship passengers to the nearby city of Vytegra on horseback. Seems it took so long for ships to pass through those old wooden locks that some passengers just got off and saddled up. Others went ashore and simply walked, picking mushrooms and berries along the way, no doubt. Devyatiny has grown over the last few decades, as families from surrounding low-lying areas moved here when hydroplant construction flooded their villages.

[KM 861–4] The **Novinkinskiy Hydroplant** consists of three separate locks: **Lock #3, Lock #4** and **Lock #5.** The combined net change in water level here is 38 meters. St. Petersburg-bound ships drop; Moscow-bound ships rise. Give or take a few centimeters, each lock measures the same: 264 x 17.8 x 19.4 meters. Those aboard ships heading to Moscow might be interested to know that their approach to Lock #3 is the only place on the canal where the ship's captain is required to take the helm personally. Somebody go and wake that guy!

[KM 864–9] Along the **Belousovskoye Reservoir** is the village of **Belousovo,** which means "White Mustache" in Russian. (Who knows why it's named that.) On the opposite shore is a statue of a woman supporting a young girl—a tribute to the wartime roles played by women.

[KM 869] Lock #2 at the **Belousovskiy Hydroplant** was opened along with Lock #1 in 1961. The net change in water level here is 12.75 meters. St. Petersburg-bound ships drop; Moscow-bound ships rise. The lock's dimensions are 270 x 17.7 x 19.4 meters.

[KM 871 sb] The wooden houses along the peninsula constitute the village of **Ankhimovo.** The deteriorating Church of Our Savior (1780), with only one cupola remaining on its five drums, stands beside a small chapel and sepulcher built by a 19th century Vytegra merchant. Between the church and the chapel formerly stood a multi-domed, multi-tiered, wooden church, conspicuously similar to the breathtaking Transfiguration Cathedral on Kizhi Island. The structure, called the Intercession Church (1708), was rumored to have been created by the same ax-wielding stud who built Kizhi's architectural wonder. The one here, unfortunately, burned to the ground in 1963.

[KM 879 sb] Boats sailing on a hidden canal appear to be cutting through the trees as you pass the city of **Vytegra.** The cupolas in the distance belong to the Purification Cathedral, built in 1869 to commemorate the city's centennial. As early as the 15th century, though, settlements here engaged in transporting goods over land from Lake

Onega to the Kovzha River. In the first half of the 19th century Vytegra
was a bustling provincial center and served as a primary port along the
newly augmented Mariinskaya System. During the second half of the
century a railway was built, the Mariinskaya System declined, and so
did the city. An observer wrote in 1860, "I have never seen a place more
lifeless and sad than Vytegra, which combines all the inconveniences of
a small and unorganized town with the deathliness of a village without
agricultural activity." Vytegra had all the makings of a splendid place of
exile, though, and hosted one of Lenin's co-conspirators, A. D. Tsurupa,
in 1903. The city retained some of its importance when the Vytegra
Hydroplant opened in the 1960s. Passengers aboard ships that stop in
Vytegra for a visit will learn all this and more while touring the amusing
exhibit located inside the Purification Cathedral. The attentive visitor
will notice the authentic Soviet organization of the exhibit—enjoy, as
these kinds of places are getting rarer and rarer. An old wooden lock from
the Mariinskaya System awaits your inspection in Vytegra as well.

[KM 880] Ships pass through **Lock #1** at the **Vytegra Hydroplant,**
which opened in 1964. The net change in water level is 13.25 meters.
St. Petersburg-bound ships drop; Moscow-bound ships rise. The lock's
dimensions are 270 x 17.8 x 19.25 meters. Constructing it was quite toil-
ful, requiring the excavation of two million cubic meters of earth and
the laying of 100,000 cubic meters of concrete. The entire chamber of
the lock, including its five-meter-thick bottom, was assembled on land
beside the old wooden Mariinskaya lock it was to replace. In town the
old wooden lock is on display along with the old lock station.

[KM 882 sb] The town of **Kirpichniy Zavod** is named after a brick plant
located here. In addition to timber piles galore, there also is a fishery
here where Lake Onega fishermen deliver their catch.

[KM 888 p] The entrance to the **Onega Canal** can be seen. There is a
sign marking the point, but unless you can decipher Old Slavonic script
you won't be able to read it.

[KM 893] The waters of **Lake Onega** officially join those of the **Vytegra
Canal.** The body of water on which the ship now sails (between locks #1

and #2) is the **Vytegra Reservoir,** a massive flood basin covering several old locks of the Mariinskaya System, now some 13 meters below. Also submerged is a hill (now an island) called Besednaya Gora, or "Discussion Mountain," where Peter the Great once had a chat with engineers about the possibility of building a canal here, as the teams of barge men, who actually pulled ships by rope from one lock to another, just weren't cutting it.

LAKE ONEGA
(KM 893-950)

[KM 893-950] Most ships don't actually sail this 57-kilometer stretch along the southern shore of **Lake Onega** (see p. 160), the distance is noted here only to preserve the kilometer tally. Instead, they typically travel some 150 kilometers northwest to the Karelian capital of **Petrozavodsk.** (see p. 117). They then cut across the lake some 55 kilometers to visit **Kizhi Island** (see p. 123) and finally head south 150 kilometers to exit the lake and continue the river navigation. Some ships simply bypass Petrozavodsk and head directly to Kizhi. Either way, the net result of this diversion is some excellent sightseeing and about 300 extra kilometers to your overall total.

SVIR RIVER
(KM 950-1166)

[KM 950] The first visible town on the Svir River (see p. 161), **Voznesenye** is named after the Ascension Monastery, which stood here for some 200 years after its founding in the 16th century. With the opening of the Onega Canal in the 19th century, Voznesenye grew substantially and now occupies both banks of the river. One bank presents an industrial face; the other maintains a provincial character, with wooden dwellings and walking paths. Residents from the pretty side commute to the ugly side on small boats and ferries. At the end of town, you pass the entrance to

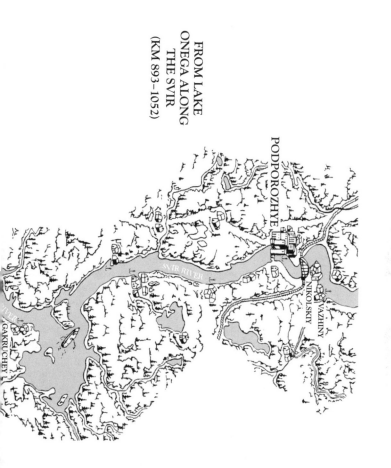

FROM LAKE
ONEGA ALONG
THE SVIR
(KM 893–1052)

the Onega Canal, a thoroughfare allowing small crafts to bypass Lake Onega when traveling between the Svir and Kovzha Rivers.

[**KM 952 sb**] You might be able see an old WWII pillbox.

[**KM 955 sb**] The village of **Chashcheruchey** can be identified by a railway-serviced pier on which river rafts are disassembled. On the opposite shore is the village **Karnavolok,** where rafts from northern rivers are reassembled to continue journeying along the Svir.

[**KM 957 p**] The settlement of **Krasniy Bor,** or "Red Grove," is distinguished by an old, Gogolesque wooden church which likely dates from the 17th or early 18th century.

[**KM 961–7 p**] A long island called **Ivanko** might be mistaken for the riverbank.

[**KM 979 sb**] In front of the village of **Gakruchey** stands a pier where passengers used to board monthly ships sailing between Nizhny Novgorod and St. Petersburg.

[**KM 982–95**] Ships operate under lake navigational conditions while cruising the 117-square-kilometer **Ivinskiy Flooded Area,** formed when engineers working on construction of the Upper Svir Hydroplant decided to flood the area without fortifications or regard for the local ecology. Wildlife you might spot around here now include duck, woodcock and white partridge. Log cabins you might spot along the shore are where St. Petersburg hunters drink vodka after shooting the wildlife. You might also notice fencing protruding a meter or so out of the water. It is designed to catch islands of peat which float around willy-nilly, creating a nuisance for ship navigators and lock operators.

[**KM 1031–3 sb**] The village on the bank is **Khevronino,** approximately 500 years old. Most of its inhabitants work in quarries or raise cattle. Many of the houses along the shores are over one hundred years old and are fine examples of architecture of the Russian north, with log foundations and sharply pitched roofs that facilitate snow runoff. If some of the dwellings look unusually large, it is because newlywed couples often build their homes to adjoin those of their parents. The entrances are on opposite sides of the house.

[KM 1034] As the banks become taller and more striking, the river bends sharply at an area called **Medvedyets Kolyeno,** or "Bear's Knee."

[KM 1040] The **Upper Svir Lock (Hydroplant)** is set amidst the shipyards, lumberyards and cargo ports of Podporozhye. On the outside of the upper lock towers, bas-relief panels depict scenes of the lock's construction. Crowning the lower towers are plaster hammer-and-sickle sculptures on which stand iron replicas of various riverships. Four different types of vessels, representing the history of river travel, are depicted: sailboat, galley, steamship and modern motorship. If your ship stays in the middle of the lock chamber, you'll find yourself face to face with a white monolith featuring a portrait of Lenin. The prominent inscription below the portrait reads, "Lenin lived, Lenin lives, Lenin will live!" Yeah, right. At any rate, the net change in water level here is 24 meters. St. Petersburg-bound ships drop; Moscow-bound ships rise. The lock's dimensions are 281 x 21.5 x 30.5 meters.

[KM 1040–7] During WWII **Podporozhye,** now spread out on both banks of the river, was a German-occupied village with more than its share of war heroes. Two of them, Anna Lisitzina, age 19, and Mariya Melentyeva, age 17, got hold of useful enemy documents and set out to deliver them to Soviet headquarters in Karelia. Crossing the Svir, Anna drowned from cramps, biting her own arm to muffle her screams. Mariya made it across and reached Soviet headquarters, after venturing through the thick Karelian forest for days. Upon returning to Podporozhye, she was promptly killed by the Germans. Another local hero, a 19-year-old nurse named Valeriya Gnarovskaya, wrapped herself in grenades and dove beneath an enemy tank during heavy fighting. Needless to say, there are quite a few memorials standing in town. Podporozhye became an established city fifty years ago during construction of the Upper Svir Hydroplant. Today it is an industrial center and headquarters to Svir River navigational dispatchers.

[KM 1047] The river is narrow here (about 100 meters across) and the current is swift. Ships cruise under a steel bridge which can be raised if the water level is too high for safe passage.

[KM 1050-2 sb] The town of **Nikolskiy** was founded by Peter the Great, who enticed Moscow Germans here for the purpose of casting chains and anchors for his wooden ships being built down the river at Lodeinoye Pole. A proper shipyard was built here in 1945 and now produces motorboats, docks and cargo cranes.

[KM 1055 sb] The town of **Vazhiny** administrates all the lumber yards along the Svir. A recently completed, railway-connected cargo port on the town's outskirts functions as an important commerce junction. You might see Volga riverboats waiting to unload their wares into train cars destined for St. Petersburg or Murmansk.

[KM 1057 sb] The ship hugs the bank at the mouth of the **Vazhinka River,** on which timber is floated just like in the old days.

[KM 1064 sb] The town of **Uslanka** was once well known for its iron foundry. Unfortunately, the foundry was flooded when the river was dammed. Now the settlement is pretty sleepy and considerably smaller than it once was.

[KM 1067-9] Two docks, on which often are piled coal and sand, stick out from the thick forest. This is a one-way section of river, tricky for navigators.

[KM 1080 p] Many ships these days call at the village of **Mandrogi.** The area was settled by Veps tribes more than a thousand years ago. More recently in history, Peter the Great's shipbuilders settled here while working at the nearby shipyard in Lodeinoye Pole. During WWII the village was completely obliterated and even disappeared from Russian maps. In 1996 Sergey Gutzeit, an entrepreneur and patron of the arts, decided to revive the village and turn it into a tourist attraction and recreational area. While here, you will be treated to a Russian style barbecue and will have ample opportunity to flex your credit cards to acquire some of the best-made Russian handicrafts of the journey, many of which are created by artisans in workshops on the premises. The village also features several cafés, a zoo, an outstanding vodka museum and a post office from which you can make easy but expensive international phone calls.

[KM 1086 p] The riverside settlement of **Svirstroy,** sprinkled with dachas, was home to all those who worked on the Lower Svir Hydroplant. Some ships make a quick "green stop" here, allowing passengers to regain their land legs.

[KM 1087] The ship enters the **Lower Svir Lock (Hydroplant),** about which Soviet sources relay an amusing anecdote. Intent on harnessing the Svir under Lenin's 1920 State Plan for the Electrization of Russia, Soviet engineers invited their American counterparts for feasibility consultations. The Americans advised against building a dam and lock at this location because of soft clay and sand at the proposed construction site. They deemed the project technologically adventurous, concluding that a dam here would sooner or later fall. Unimpressed with the American evaluation, the chief Soviet engineer proclaimed, "The station will be built, and it will work for socialism!" So in spring 1927, top Communist Party officials Kirov and Kalinin themselves came here to lay the first stones. The facility opened in 1933 and operated without incident for the next ten years. Then it indeed fell, but not of its own accord. The Soviet Army blew up the lock's gates during WWII to flood advancing German troops. After the war, the lock was rebuilt and has been working—albeit not entirely for socialism—ever since.

The net change in water level here is 12 meters. The lock's dimensions are 198 x 21.5 x 20.4 meters. Ships coming from St. Petersburg rise (and, oh yes, welcome to the first lock of your journey). Ships from Moscow drop (and that's all she wrote lockwise for your journey).

[KM 1096] The small settlement of **Yanega** lies where a river of the same name joins the Svir. The Svirskiy fish breeding grounds, whose purpose is to keep the Svir and its tributaries stocked with salmon and trout (the dam of the Lower Svir Hydroplant blocks natural spawning routes), are located here.

[KM 1098] The ship passes under the middle section of the **Lodeinopolskiy Bridge.**

[KM 1099–104 p] The ship cruises by the historical town of **Lodeinoye Pole,** spread out on the high bank. The town's name means "Boat Yard,"

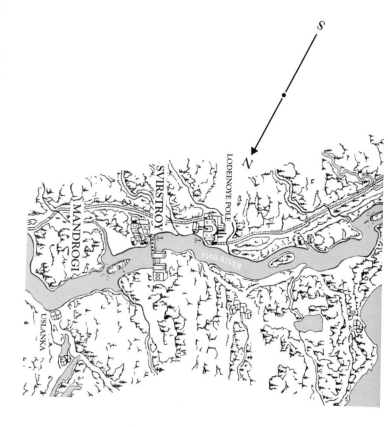

ALONG THE SVIR
TO LAKE LADOGA
(KM 1052–1315)

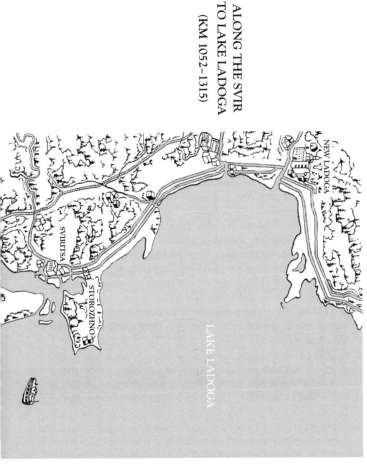

for it was here that Peter the Great instituted a large shipyard in 1702. Peter summoned his old Dutch shipbuilding buddies along with crafts-men from around Russia to build his sailing fleet. Peter's right-hand man, Alexander Menshikov, personally supervised the works, and Peter himself visited frequently to lend an expert hand. Operable well into the 19th century, the shipyard produced some 450 vessels out of local timber. After the yard closed, Lodeinoye Pole dwindled until the 1930s, at which time construction of the nearby Lower Svir Hydroplant renewed the town's importance. During WWII Lodeinoye Pole had the misfortune of lying at the front of Soviet defense lines and was pretty much destroyed. On the riverbank in the midst of a cemetery (partially eclipsed by trees) stands a commemorative statue of a soldier holding a shield.

[KM 1105 p] Timber piles awaiting river transport line the shores.

[KM 1121] A densely forested island called **Konev Island,** or "Horse Island," will be passed in this vicinity.

[KM 1127 sb] Where the **Segazha River** joins the Svir you might see a few houses constituting the villages **Gorka** and **Kofkinitsa.**

[KM 1131 sb] There is an island around here called **Gneelno;** its name derives from a Russian word applied to dangerous, remote, marshy areas. These days it's not so treacherous, but if you're here in August, there's a fair chance the ship will be waylaid by fog.

[KM 1131–47] Nothing particularly amusing here, just an austerely serene stretch of narrow river with tall, jagged banks of a reddish hue and abundant pine and fir.

[KM 1152 p] On the right bank of the **River Oyat,** which enters here, lies a row of wooden houses comprising the village of **Sermaksa,** one of the oldest on the Svir. It has a bit of a hardy history: In the 16th cen-tury, the Swedes sacked it. In the early 17th century, during the Time of Troubles, one of the False Dmitrys attempted to commandeer the place but was turned away by ax- and scythe-wielding peasants. During the 18th and 19th centuries, it served as a place of exile for political agitators. In 1907 the agitators couldn't resist agitating some more and organized a massive raftsmen strike. After the 1917 Revolution, Sermaksa played host to a more underhanded form of exile—a massive state farm named after Lenin.

[KM 1159 p] Floating in the mouth of the **Pasha River,** the settlement of **Sviritsa** spreads over eight islands around which winds the **Novosvirskiy Canal,** providing passage for ships and freighters. This important 13th century Novgorod trading port today is home to ship navigators and timber industry workers.

[KM 1159–66] This is the **Svir River** mouth. It is not clearly discernible because of its 700-meter width, which is the result of another river mouth here, that of a major Svir tributary, the **Pasha River**. This entire area is a state natural preserve, home to elk, bear, lynx and water fowl, including frequently seen gray crane. Two of the larger islands passed by the ship are **Oleniy** and **Leesiy,** or "Deer" and "Fox Islands."

LAKE LADOGA
(KM 1166–315)

[KM 1166–315] Ships operate under sea navigational conditions as they cross **Lake Ladoga** (see p. 162). "Sea navigational conditions" may sound threatening, but usually the trip is pretty smooth sailing. Usually. For those passengers whose itineraries include a stop at **Valaam Island** (see p. 129) in the northern reaches of the lake, add about 200 extra kilometers to your trip's total. Ships not diverting to Valaam will cross the southern width of the lake (149 km), passing by the lighthouse-crowned island of **Sukho,** a WWII battle monument, midway. Passengers on all ships should be able to catch a glimpse of the red-and-white lighthouse of **Storozhno,** standing in the bay near the mouth of the Svir River and resembling a tall smokestack. The lighthouse marks a settlement where, according to lore, a band of 16th century pirates were so thankful to be saved from a perilous storm that they changed their ways and founded a monastery.

NEVA RIVER
(KM 1315-69)

[KM 1315-7 p] There are several major points of interest along this stretch where the **Neva River** (see p. 163) joins **Lake Ladoga** (see p. 162). Of greatest interest is the island fortress called *Petrokrepost* by Russians but known as **Schlüsselburg** to the rest of us. Representing a typical saga of Russian naming and renaming, the island, first fortified in 1323 by Georgiy of Novgorod, was first known to the Russians as *Oreshek*, or "little nut," and to their adversaries the Swedes as *Noteburg*. The two foes bickered and killed each other over the thing until 1702, when Peter the Great captured it once and for all and named it *Schlüsselburg*, German for "Key Fortress." In 1944, when German sentiment wasn't real high, the island's name was changed to *Petrokrepost*, Russian for "Peter's Fortress," and was staunchly defended by the Soviet army for the duration of WWII.

On the mainland lies the city of Petrokrepost, or Shlisselburg, or whatever you want to call it. Aside from the massive Nevsky Shipyard, the main visible point of interest is the baroque Annunciation Cathedral, painted apricot and white yet in rather derelict shape since its closure in 1930. Along with scores of other churches, this one was returned to Orthodox hands in the government's *perestroika* rush to religious embrace.

For the 200 or so years between the Northern War and the 1917 Bolshevik Revolution, the Schlüsselburg Fortress was used as a prison and execution site for all kinds of nemeses of the tsar, ranging from Peter the Great's first wife to Lenin's brother Alexander. With a reputation that makes Alcatraz Island seem like a Sheraton, the island was converted into a revolutionary museum in the 1920s. Today, rumor has it that a specialized adventure travel firm can arrange for you to spend two weeks locked in one of the prison's old cells with nothing but pen and paper, meager meals and daily psychological check-ups just in case the ghosts believed to inhabit the thick stone walls begin to get to you.

A jetty from the mainland marks the entrances to two separate canals. The canal to the right, the **Old Ladoga Canal,** was started by the hands of Peter the Great in 1719. The tsar was tired of Svir River-bound vessels capsizing in the rough waters of Lake Ladoga—10,000 crafts went down from 1703 to 1731—and wanted a way to bypass the lake. To the left is the **New Ladoga Canal,** which was opened in 1866 to accommodate steamboats and served as the main water route to and from the Svir for the next hundred years. It is still used today by light crafts.

[KM 1319 p] As you pass the settlement of **Ugolniy** you might spot large deposits of coal awaiting river transport.

[KM 1325 p] Where the nine-section **Ladoga Bridge** joins the Neva's southern bank look out for a WWII memorial in the form of a genuine Soviet T-34 tank. Inside the bridge itself is a diorama-museum called "The Break of the Siege."

[KM 1330 p] The city of **Kirovsk** can be identified by a hydroelectric plant, smokestacks atop an old gray factory and a nursery. A statue of Kirov may or may not still be standing near the hydroelectric plant.

[KM 1332 p] A large granite pillar on the shore tributes the former town of **Arbuzovo,** which was virtually eradicated during WWII along with a substantial number of Soviet troops. Passing ships often salute by sounding their horns.

[KM 1336 p] The wooden houses amidst the trees constitute the village of **Lobanovo,** located near the mouth of the **Mga River.**

[KM 1338] The **Kuzminskiy Railway Bridge** (blown up in self-defense by Soviet troops in 1941 and rebuilt in 1954) consists of three segments, one of which should be raised to allow the ship's passage.

[KM 1341 sb] A small island called **Glav Ryba,** or "Fish Central," was once a salmon breeding grounds.

[KM 1344–6 p] The ship sails through the two-kilometer-long **Ivanovskiye Rapids.** Moscow-bound vessels are given the right-of-way in this bottleneck where the current moves at a rate of three meters per second. At the St. Petersburg end of the rapids, the **Tosna River** joins the Neva at the Otradinsky cargo port and shipyard. Spanning the mouth of the Tosna are two bridges which Soviet troops successfully defended during WWII. A stone obelisk standing in a military cemetery commemorates

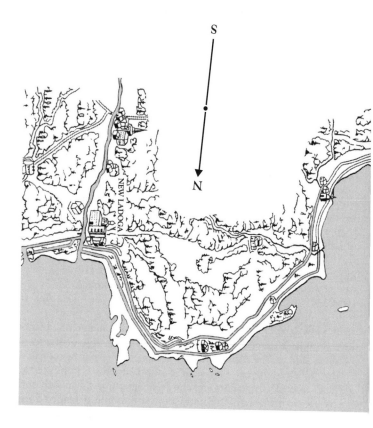

FROM LAKE LADOGA
TO ST. PETERSBURG
(KM 1315–1369)

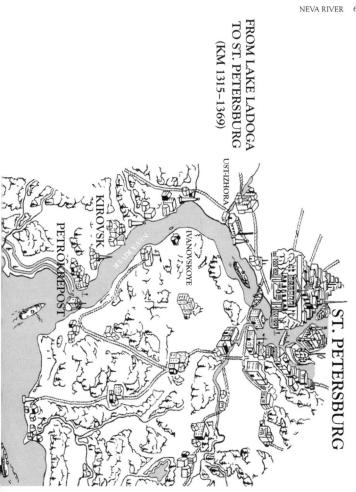

PETROKREPOST

KIROVSK

USTIZHORA

IVANOVSKOYE

NEVA MAIN

ST. PETERSBURG

the effort. On the opposite shore, an even more impressive WWII monument can be seen: a large earthen pyramid with concrete steps called "Nameless Hill" on which Soviet soldiers successfully vowed never to allow a German footprint during the war.

[KM 1353–7 p] The **Ust-Izhora** settlement lies on the Neva's southern bank where the **Izhora River** enters. A church (at last sighting under restoration) stands nearby on the site where on 15 July 1240 Russian hero Alexander Yaroslavovich, prince of Novgorod, ambushed Swedes who were planning to cross the Neva with the nasty idea of capturing the Novgorod lands. For his part in repelling the Swedes, Alexander was bestowed with the name *Nevsky*, meaning "of the Neva." He got all kinds of nice things named after him, including St. Petersburg's Alexander Nevsky Monastery, and even was canonized.

[KM 1364 sb] The settlement along the bank is **Novosaratov** ("New Saratov"), founded in the 18th century by former residents of the Volga city of Saratov. On the opposite shore lies a suburb called **Rybatskoye,** or "Fisherman's Village," where the tsar's fishermen used to reside.

[KM 1367 sb] At the St. Petersburg city line the ship navigates a wide section of river called **Utkina zavod**, where passenger ships and barges are docked for repair. A notable green industrial-like structure is the Red October thermal electricity plant. One of the first of its kind in the country, this plant alone provided electricity to the city during the WWII blockade of Leningrad. If you can pick out a building on the opposite shore that resembles a steel mill, you are likely viewing a mill called Bolshevik, where St. Petersburg's first Marxist proletarian societies were formed.

[KM 1369] Welcome to **St. Petersburg's River Passenger Terminal,** built in 1970 in typical uninspired Soviet style. Thankfully, it's a sharp contrast to what awaits you downtown.

↑ THE RIVER ROUTE ↑
**(begins here for passengers
originating in St. Petersburg)**

PORTS OF CALL

Use this section to learn about the history, population and sights of each city at which the ship casts anchor. Don't miss the sections entitled The Inside Scoop, with tips on how to make the most of organized shore excursions as well as how to most effectively strike out on your own. Cities are ordered as visited from Moscow to St. Petersburg.

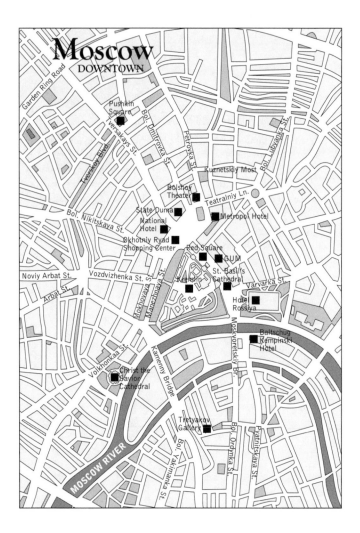

MOSCOW

ORIENTATION

Welcome to the capital of the largest country on earth, the onetime seat of an empire and command-post of global politics that is alternately considered to be Asian, European, both and neither. Almost 850 years old and currently existing amidst rapidly changing political and economic conditions, Moscow presents a dizzying array of the old and new, the alienating and quaint, the shabby and sparkling.

HISTORY

One would expect the founding of Russia's very own Mecca to be well documented, but it is not. The generally accepted version is that Suzdal Prince Yury Dolgoruky (the Long-armed) visited a village atop Borovitsky Hill (the sight of the present Kremlin) in 1147 and decided it had all the makings of a future metropolis. He returned in 1156 to build a wooden fortress, and Moscow was born.

Along with Yaroslavl, Kostroma and the rest of the Vladimir-Suzdal realm, Moscow was sacked by Mongol-Tatars in 1237-38. It rebounded quickly and became the head of its own principality in 1276 under the rule of its first prince, Daniil. Practically all the principalities of Russia at this time were vassals of the Mongol yoke, which allowed the princedoms relative independence so long as they functioned as dutiful tax-collecting agencies. As his name would suggest, Prince Ivan the Moneybags was quite adept at the game and was given the title Grand Prince of Muscovy in 1328. Soon thereafter Muscovy absorbed the Vladimir and Suzdal principalities on its way to becoming the center of the empire for the next 400 years.

Although the Mongols burned Moscow down in 1382 as a little revenge for their defeat by Dmitry Donskoy at Kulikovo two years earlier, their empire fell into enough disarray by the 15th century for Ivan III (the Great) to shirk Mongol domination and establish Moscow as the official capital of the Russian lands. In order to create a capital so awe-inspiring that "reality would embody fantasy on an unearthly scale," Ivan invited Pskov and Italian architects to rebuild the old wooden kremlin in stone. By 1495 they had completed the walls and towers. Ivan must have been amazed at the "New Constantinople" that had been created by his Russo-Italian team. New cathedrals were commissioned, squares laid and decorative gardens planted throughout the city. Moscow became the beautiful "big village" that it is patronizingly referred to today by non-Muscovites.

Ivan the Great's grandson Ivan IV (the Terrible) was born in the Kremlin and had himself crowned tsar (the first to assume the title) within its walls at age 16. Ivan married seven times, killed off most of his boyars and slew his own eldest son in a fit of rage, but saved historical face by "gathering the Russian lands." Although it was his grandfather who united most of the principalities, it was Ivan IV who captured the Golden Horde khanates of Kazan and Astrakhan, thereby claiming the entire Volga region for Russia. He was so proud of conquering once mighty Kazan that he commemorated the feat by commissioning the construction of stupendous St. Basil's Cathedral in Moscow.

Polish forces occupied Moscow from 1610 to 1612, the peak of the Time of Troubles. They were driven out by a Volga-region army led by a mayor named Minin and a prince named Pozharsky, whose bronze likenesses today stand in front of St. Basil's Cathedral. Young boyar Michael Romanov emerged from the anarchy to take the throne, kicking off a dynasty that was to turn its back on Moscow for much of its 300-year reign by ruling from St. Petersburg, a place that was still only a swamp at the time of Michael's death in 1645.

Moscow's fall from grace began with the rule of Peter the Great (1696-1725). The sedulous young tsar resented Moscow for being too Russian. He thought the country would be more easily Westernized from the Gulf of Finland, which is where he began building his new capital, St. Petersburg. Peter's "window on the West" officially wrested the governing powers from Moscow in 1712. Because Peter compelled

THE MOSCOW NORTHERN RIVER TERMINAL

ST. BASIL'S CATHEDRAL ON RED SQUARE

THE KREMLIN WALLS ON THE MOSCOW RIVER EMBANKMENT

THE ANNUNCIATION CATHEDRAL INSIDE THE KREMLIN

the country's important figures to inhabit the new capital, it began to assume a cosmopolitan air while Moscow took a humbling back seat.

Napoleon, a romantic sort who didn't care if Moscow was no longer the capital, focused his campaign of 1812 on the capture of the ancient city, a feat he pulled off fairly easily, notwithstanding some admirable Russian resistance at Borodino. Spending his first gleeful night in the Kremlin, the French commander went to sleep thinking his war was won. Soon, however, he began to wonder why no declaration of Russian capitulation was arriving. He realized that the entire city population had left him and his troops to brave the upcoming Moscow winter on their own. Never before having faced such tactics, which sort of took the fun out of the conquering business, he hastily retreated, burning down most of the city but failing to topple the mighty Kremlin itself.

Even Tolstoy, who wrote that "it would be difficult to explain what caused the Russians, after the departure of the French in 1812, to throng to the place that had been known as Moscow," was amazed by the alacrity with which the city recovered. The revival was fostered primarily by large-scale industrial expansion, which meant that the city's beloved gardens gave way to smoke-belching factories and shabby suburbs sprung up to house the influx of workers.

The Bolsheviks overcame savage street fighting in October 1917 to capture the Kremlin en route to achieving their coup d'etat. In March 1918, with Soviet power declared across the country, Lenin and his Bolsheviks brought the capital back to Moscow. The party of the working class took up its operations within the ancient walls of the historical seat of royalty. "Necessary dictatorship" was established as a temporary transitional measure. It became, however, a permanent way of governing.

After Lenin passed away in 1924 the city was virtually raped by irresponsible leaders, most notably a mustachioed monster named Josef Stalin. Using an army of cost-efficient labor (GULAG prisoners) and liberal amounts of TNT, the notorious champion of progress went about redesigning the capital to have it more appropriately reflect the triumphant march of socialism. As outlined in the General Plan for the

Reconstruction of Moscow, thousands of historical and architectural monuments were blown up, including the famed Church of Christ the Savior (totally rebuilt in 1997). Streets were straightened and widened, neighborhoods demolished and seven ominous "Stalinist Gothic" skyscrapers sprung up around the Garden Ring Road. By the time of Stalin's death in 1953, a full half of Moscow's historical and architectural monuments had been turned to dust. The new alienating city layout, designed to flout pomp, drained the ancient capital of charm and cleansed it of traditional Russian character. It was a feat that likely would have made Peter the Great proud.

During the Khrushchev years (1957-64), Moscow's outskirts became littered with *khrushchevky*, hastily built residential projects resembling concrete blocks. The Brezhnev years were characterized by stagnation, except for a brief period in 1980, when in preparation for the Olympic Games, Moscow gained a few stadiums and hotels and swept its dirt under the carpet. Privatization sparked by Mikhail Gorbachev's *perestroika* resulted in the renovation of some world-class hotels and the appearance of swanky restaurants, clubs and casinos, which go in and out of business depending on their popularity and Mafia protection. As we set off into the 21st century, Moscow has increasingly come to resemble a bustling Eurasian metropolis, as omnipresent kiosks, street traders and now, luxury malls and department stores stake their claim to Russia's furious fledgling capitalism.

ABOUT THE CITY

That first-time visitors as well as lifelong Muscovites so easily overlook evidence of the city's destructive history is not surprising, so extraordinary and diverse are Moscow's attributes. Although ascribing the city's allure to its having one foot in Asia and one in Europe is an overused cop-out, when you find yourself standing on Teatralnaya Ploshchad surrounded by the classical presence of the Bolshoy Theater, the Art Deco touches of the Metropol Hotel and the Byzantine imposition of the Kremlin towers, you certainly feel amidst a fairy tale whose origins are elusive.

In any Russian city the word *tsentr* (center) is used to denote the downtown area; throughout the country at large, *tsentr* also refers to Moscow itself, the center of everything in Russia. Political coups, theatrical debuts, scientific revelations and fashion trends all originate in the country's capital. With some 2,500 historical and architectural monuments, 70 museums, 125 cinemas, 50 theaters, 4,500 libraries, 540 higher educational and research institutions (including the oldest university in the country) and a labyrinth of back streets, secluded neighborhoods and sprawling suburbs, the city can only be properly explored over a lifetime.

The populace of Russia's largest city are engaged in a variety of industries, including metalworking, oil refining, automobile manufacturing, chemical, wood, and paper processing, film production, tourism and lately, good old fashioned wholesale/retail. At last count, Moscow's population was around nine million people, who consume an average of two million bottles of vodka per day.

SIGHTS

You'll hear the exclamation "*oy!*" a lot in Russia—whenever someone stubs a toe, nearly runs into a car or faces a task of daunting proportions, such as enumerating all the possible sights of interest in Moscow. With a friendly "*oy!*" the author hereby advises the reader to consult any of the numerous comprehensive Moscow city guidebooks to get a full overview of the city's sights. Below you will find descriptions of the destinations usually covered by ships' shore excursions, including a section called The Inside Scoop, with inside tips.

The Kremlin

"Towers of every form, round, square, and with pointed roofs, belfries, donjons, turrets, spires, sentry boxes upon minarets, steeples of every height, style and colour, palaces, domes, watchtowers, walls, embattlemented and pierced with loopholes, ramparts, fortifications of every species, whimsical inventions, incomprehensible devices, chiosks by the sides of cathedrals..." [*sic*]

Such was the initial impression of the Moscow Kremlin upon the rather disparaging consciousness of the Marquis de Custine, who toured Russia in 1839. Although the function of several of the Kremlin's structures may have changed since then, the presence of the most breathtaking citadel on earth has not. The Kremlin is the legacy of Ivan the Great, who rebuilt a fortress that was here at the end of the 15th century. "But," states Custine, "if this place was not built by Ivan the Terrible, it was built for him"—an allusion to the despotism that many have ascribed to the awesome architecture itself. Indeed, within the Kremlin walls Ivan the Terrible fashioned his tyranny, Napoleon watched the city burn, Lenin redirected his revolution toward dictatorship, Stalin barked his genocidal commands and Brezhnev snored while his country fell decades behind the West.

The only treachery facing the modern day visitor to the Kremlin is all the swarming summer tourist groups. But it's worth it to bear the crowds, as the structures within the Kremlin comprise the historical heart and soul of Russia.

The white limestone **Assumption Cathedral,** its five gilded cupolas glittering atop narrow drums, stood for centuries as the national shrine of Russia. Before its altar tsars were crowned and patriarchs anointed. Even after the seat of the monarchy was moved to St. Petersburg, new sovereigns, including the last tsar, doomed Nicholas II, journeyed to Moscow to officially commence their reign here. Empress Elizabeth used up 800 horses to pull her carriage here from St. Petersburg in 1741. Of the cathedral's interior, Custine, who naturally was biased toward the gothic likes of Chartres, remarked, "The church is nearly square, very lofty, and so small that on walking in it you feel as if in a dungeon." (Was it mentioned he was disparaging?) Rumor has it that the cathedral houses a collection of holy relics that includes one of the nails driven through Jesus of Nazareth's wrists. The exterior of the building, dating from 1475, can be characterized as Byzantine with Renaissance touches. Napoleon used the cathedral as a horse stable and some of its icons for firewood while he graced the Kremlin with his presence in 1812.

The **Annunciation Cathedral,** built in the late 1500s, served for centuries as personal shrine of the tsars. These days it boasts an unequaled collection of significant icons, many rendered by Theophanes the Greek, considered one of the finest of all icon painters. The cathedral was originally a simple, three-domed affair, but Ivan the Terrible added six more cupolas, four chapels and a dazzling gilded roof. He also commissioned the construction of a side entrance for his personal use, as he was forbidden by the patriarch to use the main entrance because of the tsar's penchant for divorcing his wives.

Across from the Annunciation Cathedral stands the five-domed **Archangel Michael Cathedral,** built in 1505-08. The interior is dominated by sarcophagi containing the remains of practically every Russian tsar up to the reign of Peter the Great. The tomb of Ivan the Terrible rests behind the iconostasis. Those who have already visited the site of the murder of Ivan's son Dmitry in Uglich might be interested to know that the young saint is resting more or less peacefully here beneath a painted stone canopy.

At the edge of the Kremlin you gain entrance to Russia's oldest and most fascinating museum, the **State Armory Chamber.** Try not to think about the oppression endured by the Russian people throughout the ages as you saunter past Boris Godunov's throne, encrusted with 2,000 precious stones; Alexey Romanov's throne, adorned with 1,000 diamonds; or Catherine the Great's coronation crown, covered with pearls and 5,000 diamonds. These imperial toys are just the tip of the iceberg. Prepare yourself for gold and silver galore—chalices, bowls, goblets, jewelry—as well as royal vestments, robes and headdresses. The Armory houses the world's largest collection of carriages, which is displayed in one stupendous room alive with gilded swirls of baroque and rococo monsters the likes of which you've never imagined. And there's also the 189-carat Orlov Diamond that Count Orlov gave to his mistress, Catherine the Great. Fabergé eggs are often exhibited here, but they have a tendency to move around, so you'll have to ask your guide how to track them down to behold their miracles.

Besides the four above-mentioned destinations the only other sights your local guide is sure to walk you past while within the Kremlin are the 40-ton **Tsar Cannon,** the largest cannon in the world (never fired), and the 210-ton **Tsar Bell,** the largest bell in the world (never rung).

Red Square

Among the most famous metropolitan squares in the world, this is where you really feel like you're in Russia. Here government decrees were read, tsars' opponents slaughtered, potatoes and vodka bartered and Soviet leaders dutifully tributed by their subjects during government sham pageants. This is also where young German pilot Mathias Rust cheekily landed his Cessna in 1987, causing the Soviet government a wee bit of embarrassment. You can bet *he* really felt like he was in Russia when he got out of the plane.

Cobblestone throughout its 70,000 square meter expanse (the stones are from a quarry near Lake Onega), Red Square is bordered by the Kremlin wall, St. Basil's Cathedral, GUM department store and the multi-gabled, red-brick State Historical Museum.

The square is still oriented around the famed **Lenin Mausoleum,** lying in front of the Kremlin wall. Visitors in 1993 were the last to witness the spectacle of the tomb's goose-stepping guards changing every hour, but you can still venture inside to experience the other-worldliness of the mausoleum's dark interior. No one knows where Lenin ultimately will end up, but the government has contemplated sending him on a world tour and/or relocating him to St. Petersburg next to his mother's grave, according to his wishes. They better hurry, though, as poor Lenin shrinks a few centimeters each year and is known to sprout fungi from time to time.

Exiting the mausoleum, you proceed through a **memorial walk** along the Kremlin wall. This is the final resting place of a motley crew of Soviet leaders, some of whose ashes lie in urns within the Kremlin wall. Pay your respects to the likes of Chernenko, Andropov, Brezhnev, Dzerzhinsky, Kirov, Sverdlov and the most infamous of all, Stalin, who judging by the abundance of flowers on his slab is still loved despite having systematically exterminated 30 million of his countrymen. More neutral figures honored here include cosmonaut Yury Gagarin, Soviet writer Maxim Gorky and misguided American journalist John Reed.

What really captivates the visitor to Red Square, of course, is the orgy of multi-colored onion domes that is **St. Basil's Cathedral.** Despite being exploited by travel posters, guidebook covers, and satellite broadcasts, the image of Russia's signature monument somehow transcends itself and captivates visitors as if never seen before. Considered the embodiment of traditional Russian architecture, the structure in fact is a deviation from convention, consisting of nine connected chapels organized on a fairly simple layout. The legend that guides like to tell about Ivan the Terrible gouging out the eyes of the cathedral's architect so that his *chef-d'œuvre* could never be repeated is entertaining and surely in line with Ivan's reputation but, alas, untrue. The two architects that built the original structure actually went on to add a chapel to it four years after Ivan's death.

Opposite the Kremlin wall sprawls the facade of Russia's largest shopping center, **GUM.** Pronounced "goom," the name originally was an acronym for State Department Store. Now, having been taken over by a private company, the store advertises its initials as standing for Main Department Store (the words for *state* and *main* start with the same letter in Russian). Designed in 1895 to house 200 trading stalls, the structure was completely rebuilt in the 1950s and at its peak handled half a million customers daily. Now, with the prices of much of its wares out of reach to most Russians, the crowds have dwindled, allowing you to stroll in peace and enjoy the ornate interior, resplendent with walking bridges, fountains and a glass-paneled roof. Anyone who visited GUM before the 1990s will be shocked to see European luxury outlets such as Dior, Moschino, Vuitton and Escada occupying spaces formerly containing rows of barren state-owned stalls.

The **State Historical Museum** faces St. Basil's Cathedral from across the square. The multi-spired building was constructed in the late 1800s on the sight of the original Moscow University, founded in 1755.

Containing an exhaustive exhibit of historical artifacts ranging from manuscripts, books and coins to Peter the Great's sled and Napoleon's saber, the exhibition is an attempt to document Russian history since the Stone Ages.

The Arbat (Arbat Street)

The Arbat is a stop on the Moscow shore excursion itinerary because it offers the type of environment that tourists love: a cobblestone pedestrian thoroughfare full of shops and cafés that, in spite of its crowds, somehow seems more manageable to Westerners than most other parts of Moscow. But the Arbat is also a historic heart, a onetime entrance into the Muscovy capital, a 16th century home to courtiers and a 19th century neighborhood of aristocrats, artists and writers.

The Arbat formerly encompassed an area that is now divided into the New Arbat (*Noviy Arbat*) and the Old Arbat (simply *Arbat*). The quaint pedestrian shopping zone is the Old Arbat and is along Arbat Street. The New Arbat is along Noviy Arbat Street, which was laid by bulldozing the Arbat's original main square, a monastery and half a dozen churches. A recommended route is to walk down the old Arbat and then return via the New Arbat.

The old Arbat Street stretches from the yellow building containing the Praga restaurant to the unmistakable Foreign Ministry skyscraper. It is probably the easiest place in the city for tourists to snack, shop and people-watch. From time to time allow your attention to drift away from the street performers to the colorful facades of the old merchant houses. Collectors can find rare books and antiques along Arbat Street; the homesick can find relief at the Hard Rock Cafe and Baskin-Robbins.

The New Arbat also offers a promenade, on the south side of the wide Noviy Arbat boulevard, which takes you past sprawling casino complexes and shopping malls not generally frequented by tourists. Moscow's famed House of Books (*Dom knigi*) still is hanging onto its location on the north side of the street.

THE INSIDE SCOOP

There obviously is quite a bit to be scooped in a city the size of Moscow. Again, using a dedicated city guidebook can be helpful if the ship's program isn't to your liking or if you're spending a few extra days here. Local publications that can shed some light on current happenings and hot spots include the daily English-language newspaper *Moscow Times* and periodicals such as *Where*.

Moscow shore excursions are reviewed below. The distance between the Northern River Terminal and downtown area is great, so you are put on a bus for all tours and forays into town. Some people will be more than satisfied to go on all the guided excursions, some will want to pick and choose and others might elect to avoid them altogether. Whenever you do strike out on your own, don't forget that the tour buses can offer free and easy transportation into town. Also bear in mind that groups sometimes are shuttled back to the ship for lunch, a process that consumes as much as two to three hours and might warrant skipping.

Organized Shore Excursions

An excursion always offered by ships is the **City Tour.** It is a good outing for anyone who wants to get a general overview of Moscow and doesn't mind doing so from the inside of a chartered bus. You are let off the bus occasionally to serve as bait for souvenir-vending vultures. You will pass every point of interest in the city; your task is to try to maintain your bearings. In general, a very touristy thing to do, but a very useful one.

The **Kremlin Tour** is the one excursion not to be missed. Individual admission to the Kremlin oftentimes can be restricted and/or difficult; therefore you possess a distinct advantage being with a sanctioned group. Moreover, this outing usually includes a visit to the spectacular Armory Chamber. It's a whirlwind tour of the exhibition, but it's the only one you'll get that's devoid of major admission hassles.

A visit to **Red Square** is sometimes included in the City Tour, sometimes in the Kremlin Tour, and sometimes added to another excursion. Because of its central location, Red Square can easily be made part of your own personal outing, which might include shopping at GUM or a swanky dinner in the Metropol Hotel's famous dining room.

Occasionally a **Moscow by Night Tour** is offered. It is recommended, as Moscow by night presents an altogether different picture than by day. Floodlit Red Square, for example, with St. Basil's Cathedral looming as if from an alien fairy tale, presents an unforgettable travel memory. (Note that using a camera on a tripod is forbidden in and around Red Square.)

A **Metro Tour** is sometimes conducted. Your guide will simply herd your group underground to travel on the subway. It sounds a bit strange, but the Moscow Metro is unique in that its stations are clean and elaborately decorated with socialist artwork ranging from mosaics to sculptures to stained glass. The physical depth of the stations, lightning fast escalators and unbelievable size of the aggressive crowds add to the spectacle. If you're not the type to use the metro on your own during your stay, you owe it to yourself to tour it once. Those who might travel by metro on their own a few times should probably forego the group tour.

The **Arbat Tour** isn't really a tour at all, but rather a bus ride to Arbat Street, where you are set free for shopping. If you don't relish the idea of making an en masse tourist *entrée*, or if you want to linger in the Arbat longer than the allotted time (perhaps for a meal), then you might pass on one or both bus rides and utilize the convenient Arbat metro stations or waiting taxicabs.

Some ships offer a **Sergiev Posad (Zagorsk) Tour.** This excursion entails a day trip by bus to the environs of Moscow to visit Russia's most famous Golden Ring destination, the Trinity Monastery of St. Sergius in the town of Sergiev Posad (formerly Zagorsk). Advice on this one is tough. On one hand, you certainly see more than enough monasteries during the river voyage. On the other hand, the Trinity Monastery is the mother of all Russian monasteries. The monastery itself is absolutely breathtaking, the surroundings, including a lovely park, are serene and offer potential for a lakeside picnic and the four-hour roundtrip bus ride provides a chance to survey the outer-Moscow landscape. Then again, four hours on a bus is four hours on a bus.

Other Possibilities

Popular destinations that are easily accessible and often not included in shore excursions include the following.

Tretyakov Gallery (metro: Tretyakovskaya). The wondrous art collection of brothers Pavel and Sergey Tretyakov is housed in an early 20th century building designed to resemble a small boyar's castle. Extensively renovated and upgraded in the early 1990s, Russia's most renowned art gallery is now among its most user-friendly. For the ruble equivalent of about $10, you can rent English-language audio guides to conduct you through moving Shishkin landscapes, ancient icons and Ivanov's colossal garish masterpiece, *Christ Appearing to the People.* Closed Mondays.

Gorky Park (metro: Park Kultury). Tour groups from the ship occasionally attend the tented circus in Gorky Park. You usually are not given the time to walk around the park itself, however, which is a pity. Spending an afternoon in Gorky Park is an opportunity to glimpse Russian-style recreation. With scenic lakes, bridges, gardens, a fun zone, outdoor cafés serving *shashlik* and beer and now even bungee jumping, there's something here for everyone.

Izmailovsky Park (metro: Izmailovsky Park). The biggest weekend flea market in Moscow. All of your souvenir needs, from kitsch to valuable lacquer boxes to Soviet cameras to icons, can be met here in one mad shopping spree. Bargain hard, take a big bag, be Zen.

Kuznetskiy Most (metro: Kuznetskiy Most). Formerly aristocratic shopping grounds within walking distance of Red Square, this centrally located neighborhood makes for delightful wanderings. Walk along the main street (Kuznetskiy Most) to encounter tasty street food, fashionable clothing shops, an English language bookstore and the TSUM department store, which plays Harvey Nichols to GUM's Harrod's. Before ending in Tverskaya Street, the street transforms into Kamergerskiy Lane, a pedestrian restaurant row where Muscovites of all kinds while away the hours over coffee, beer, snacks or haute cuisine.

Tverskaya Street. As long as you have reached Tverskaya, carve out at least an hour to stroll Moscow's counterpart to Petersburg's famous Nevsky Prospekt. The street will surely look familiar to you because it is along this thoroughfare that the tour bus takes you between the port and downtown numerous times during your stay. The stretch of road between the National Hotel at the bottom of Tverskaya and Pushkin Square bustles the most. Don't forget to stop into the splendid Eliseyevskiy Market at number 14.

Okhotniy Ryad Mall (metro: Okhotniy Ryad). Moscow's first Western-style shopping mall, opened in 1998. Actually spiffier than most in the West, this occasionally crowded underground complex with lovely grounds overhead will satisfy the most discerning mallaholic. Entrances to the place are hard to find if you don't read Russian, but if you use the entrance located directly across from the Tomb of the Unknown Soldier (in the Alexandrovskiy Garden along the Kremlin's western wall), you will gain access via the mall's most distinctive pub, The Phlegmatic Dog. Here, a computer terminal at every table gives visitors unlimited access to the Internet so long as they order something, no matter how small, from the menu (which also is done via the tabletop terminal, precluding you from having to mutter any Russian at all).

Rechnoy Vokzal. Got some free time before the ship leaves Moscow? Why not take a walk through the river terminal grounds and across the highway to the Rechnoy Vokzal (River Station) metro station. The locals in the park sitting on benches love watching foreign tourists walk by, and once you reach the metro station, you can avail yourself of a small farmer's market, a plethora of kiosks and a brand new modest shopping mall. This is your chance to stock up on last-minute supplies for the cruise on the cheap.

DINING IN MOSCOW

Moscow consistently rates among the most expensive cities in the world to visit, and when you dine out, you'll see why. But hey, this is no reason not to try a few places. Hold onto the bill, and you will have something to brag about.

Bosco Café (in GUM on Red Square at Krasnaya Ploshchad 3). Only here and a few doors down at the Bosco Bar can one repose right on Red Square and enjoy a drink or a meal. Don't be fooled by the casual appearance of the Bosco Café. Some of the finest cuisine in Moscow is to be found here, including the best salads in Russia, arguably the best risotto anywhere, grilled fish, accomplished cocktails, first-rate wines, etc. Go for lunch or for dinner, and be ready to pay handsomely for the impeccable food, solid service and unmatched view.

Conservatory (in the Park Hyatt Ararat, at Neglinnaya 4). The Hyatt's rooftop terrace bar/restaurant is unbeatable for its panoramic view of Moscow and its casual yet stylish atmosphere. Although the menu presents "light meals," the portions of the artistically prepared and presented dishes are generous. Bring your camera and your appetite and forget about your budget.

Praga (Arbat Street 2). Here is your chance to sample traditional Russian fine dining, complete with *zakusksi* (traditional appetizers), sturgeon, caviar, grilled meats, dark breads and, of course, vodka. Especially good for groups.

Starlite Diner (on the Garden Ring Road, just off Tverskaya at Bolshaya Sadovaya 16). If you've got to do burgers and milkshakes at least once while in Russia, this is the place. Open 24 hours.

Shwartzwald (across from the Marriott Aurora, at Petrovskaya 14). This well-known beer restaurant manages to be modern, expansive and cozy all at once. With all the best European and Russian beers on tap and a menu of tasty treats, this is the place to whet your whistle in downtown Moscow. For something completely different, try either the Yakitori or Acapulco restaurants, located on either side of Shwartzwald.

TGI Friday's (a variety of locations, including outside Tverskaya metro station in the Izvestia building and at Noviy Arbat 14). We're not actually recommending that you come all the way to Moscow to dine at Friday's, but if you'd like a decent American-style salad or some chicken wings, we understand.

Yolki Palki (in the area of Kuznetskiy Most, at Neglinnaya 8/10). Named after a colorful Russian exclamation, this place offers traditional provincial Russian cuisine at its best, including a large salad bar of fresh and pickled appetizers, brown bread, hot soups and draught beer served in mugs. Get ready to eat some dill.

ACCOMMODATIONS IN MOSCOW

So you think restaurants in Moscow are expensive? Outside of perhaps Tokyo, you will nowhere pay more for a luxury hotel than in Moscow. While relatively affordable mid-range and budget lodgings are available, they simply cannot be recommended with a straight face.

Baltshug Kempinski (Balshug street 1). Everything you would expect from a Kempinski hotel is here, just across the Moscow River with stunning views on the Kremlin and St. Basil's Cathedral—if you pony up for a riverside room. Just don't look at the prices, and you will have a lovely time.

Metropol (Teatralniy proyezd 1/4). This is the famous classic Art Deco hotel whose hey-day was the early 1900s but whose recent refurbishing has done it well. Stay here for the large rooms, high ceilings and period pieces—and of course for the location, right across the street from the Bolshoy Theater and around the corner from Red Square.

National (Okhotniy Ryad 14/1). Recently taken over by Le Meridien and now officially called Le Royal Meridien National, this is another historic Moscow address whose location, right at the bottom of Tverskaya facing the Kremlin, cannot be beat. You pay handsomely for the privilege of staying in the stately rooms, which can be small and/or dark, so make sure you see your lodgings before you plunk down.

Park Hyatt Ararat (Neglinnaya 4). Smile politely at old-time expats telling you the Metropol and the National are the best hotels in Moscow—then get yourself to the unequivocal champion, opened in 2003. With the best rooftop terrace in the city, a gorgeous spa and fresh sushi awaiting you at all hours of the day in the lobby, there simply is no comparison to this slice of modern elegance located ideally between Kuznetskiy Most and the Kremlin.

Rossiya (Varvarka Street 6). This Soviet-era behemoth must be the largest hotel in the world, despite what the MGM Grand in Las Vegas claims. Actually, the two have some things in common: 24-hour casino and bar, thugs and pretty girls perpetually hanging around and plenty of other diversions. If you can score a room facing Red Square, you will have one of the best views available in Moscow.

Royal Marriott Aurora (Petrovka 11/20). The best located of Moscow's Marriotts, right in the Kuznetskiy Most neighborhood and close to, well, everything. Marriotts abroad tend to be leaps and bounds better than their counterparts in the States, and this spiffy hotel is no exception.

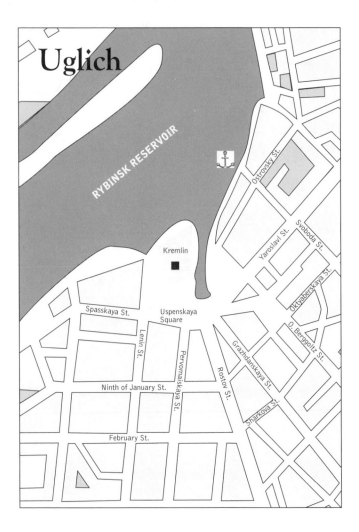

Uglich

RYBINSK RESERVOIR

Ostrovsky St.

Yaroslavi St.

Svoboda St.

Oktyaberskaya St.

O. Berggoltz St.

Kremlin

Spasskaya St.

Uspenskaya
Square

Lenin St.

Pervomaiskaya St.

Grazhdanskaya St.

Rostov St.

Sharkova St.

Ninth of January St.

February St.

THE MOSCOW CANAL LANDSCAPE

TRANSFIGURATION CATHEDRAL IN THE UGLICH KREMLIN

UGLICH'S FAMOUS CHURCH OF ST. DMITRY ON THE BLOOD

MOTHER VOLGA

UGLICH

ORIENTATION
A 1916 Volga guidebook remarks, "The city of Uglich is not in the present; it all lives in the past." Unfortunately, not much has changed here since 1916, which means that Uglich, historically located on the right bank of the Volga but now on the bank of a reservoir, features a renowned ancient kremlin in a very provincial setting.

HISTORY
In 937 an envoy of Kievan Prince Igor visited a Slavonic trading settlement on the high right bank of the Volga to "register the population." In other words, Prince Igor decided it was time to familiarize the Slavs with the concept of taxation, and he sent a representative to make the arrangement legitimate by founding a town. The Slavs were not amused. They tied Prince Igor between two bent trees and let them—and him—rip. So goes the embellished legend of the origin of Uglich.

The town's officially recognized founding is 1148, the date it was first mentioned in the Chronicles. Its name is explained by three separate theories: it is derived from the Russian word *ugol*, meaning "angle," for the Volga makes a sharp bend at Uglich; it is derived from *ugol*, which also means "coal," for coal was burned here; it is derived from the name of the town's original settlers, a Finno-Ugric tribe purportedly called *Uglichy*.

Established as its own principality in 1218 yet controlled by the Rostov–Suzdal principality throughout the 13th century, the popular Volga port thrived despite being sacked a couple of times by the pesky Mongol-Tatars. In 1326 Moscow Grand Prince Ivan (the Moneybags) purchased the flourishing principality for Muscovy. Under the 15th century rule of Prince Andrey (the Big), Uglich reached the peak of its prosperity. Its kremlin was fortified with formidable wooden walls protecting a palace complex, a monastery, a cathedral and a trading bazaar. The small principality even minted its own currency. A fire in 1491 devoured most of the wooden kremlin.

In 1552 Uglich bustled with activity as carpenters here assembled a portable wooden fortress for Ivan the Terrible to take to Kazan for use in his successful campaign against the Tatars.

In 1591 occurred the definitive event in Uglich's history: the death of Ivan the Terrible's only living heir, Dmitry. It was widely believed that Boris Godunov orchestrated Dmitry's murder, and a group of Uglich townspeople got in big trouble for killing several of Godunov's henchmen when a tribunal ruled that the tsarevich's death was due to his having an epileptic seizure while playing with a knife.

Whatever really happened, Dmitry's death sparked a power struggle for the throne, initially won by Godunov. Godunov's death in 1605 then set in motion the chaos known as the Time of Troubles. (The False Dmitrys mentioned so often in connection with the Time of Troubles were actually pretenders to the throne alleging to be grown-up Tsarevich Dmitry, miraculously not murdered after all.) Foreign armies took advantage of the political instability and headed toward Moscow. A bulwark for the capital, Uglich fell under repeated attack by the Poles and ultimately was obliterated in 1611 by the Swedes.

Resilient as ever, Uglich gradually recovered. By the end of the 17th century it had become a destination of religious pilgrimage owing to the new Church of St. Dmitry on the Blood, built to honor the slain tsarevich, since canonized. New kremlin walls, this time of stone, were built along with the church. The Transfiguration Cathedral was added to the complex in 1713, one year before Peter the Great forbid stone buildings anywhere but in St. Petersburg. Peter's other decrees nonetheless took their toll on Uglich's development. The city's bells were melted to forge artillery for the Northern War with Sweden, and the male population was summoned to St. Petersburg to either enlist in the navy or help construct stone buildings in the new capital.

Some fifty years after Peter's reign, Russia's second most fervent Westernizer, Catherine the Great, visited Uglich. The empress was greatly impressed but nonetheless ordered the town's layout changed to become more symmetrical (i.e., more European). Uglich complied with the imperial request, adding neoclassical civic structures, stone churches and stone dwellings to its newly straightened streets. (Peter's prohibition on stone structures had been lifted by this time.)

The 19th century ushered in the decline of Uglich. Additions to the Mariinskaya Canal System altered the dynamics of river travel such that ships stopped at Rybinsk, to the northeast, rather than at Uglich. Not connected to commercial centers by railway, Uglich saw one half of its enterprises fail and a large portion of its population migrate to more active areas. Yet as the century wore on, the city of uncommon beauty and rich history began to lure artists, writers and historians, who fueled a revival of Uglich's heritage. In spite of economic decline, cultural institutions were established, among them a new local studies museum and library. Mikhail Chekhov, brother of the famous writer, took up residence in the town and founded a theatrical society.

Four years prior to the 1917 Revolution, a city guidebook remarked, "Uglich is a sleepy town on the Volga River. Its glory is over, and it is difficult to believe that life will start here again." The Soviet government thought otherwise. Stalin's second and third five-year plans (1935-40) called for the implementation of a hydroplant at Uglich as part of the overall program to harness the Volga for hydroelectricity. Uglich suddenly became the base for a large-scale engineering undertaking. The city also gained a stone-cutting plant and cheese manufactory.

The reality of Uglich's 20th century revival, though, is best described by a post-*glasnost* city guidebook: "Unfortunately, the town also lost a great deal. Half of its churches were demolished, monastery walls were taken down, which detracted greatly from the appearance of the ensemble, and the old Monastery of the Intercession, with some unique monuments of the 15th, 16th and 17th centuries, was blown up and flooded. The huge building of the hydropower station was erected in its place."

In 1952, with Stalin mercifully one year away from death, a so-called restoration unit was set up in Uglich to save the town's monuments from further destruction and neglect. This was Soviet bureaucracy at its best, as the unit achieved, well, nothing. It sat by and watched while several unsightly five-story modern constructions were placed in the middle of the town center and thoughtless alterations were made to many historic structures. Recently a new general plan for the development of Uglich was adopted, calling for conservation zones and building regulations.

ABOUT THE CITY

Unlike the traveling peasantry of Kostroma, citizens of Uglich are historically characterized by a love of domesticity. The town's 19th century decline was attributed by some observers to the populace's tradition of trading amongst themselves without much interest in the outside world and without much profit.

Domestic people are dedicated and driven though, and indeed Uglichers have continued to maintain the various industries established here in the early 20th century. Aside from machine-building and jobs related to the operation of the Uglich Hydroplant, the citizenry are involved in cheese-making and watch-manufacturing. The Chaika watch factory hammers out five million timepieces a year in a plant at the edge of town.

Denizens of Uglich are also known to take advantage of the surrounding countryside, still endowed with coniferous forests in spite of industrial exploitation. An excerpt from a recent local guidebook paints a more vivid picture with characteristic wryness: "In spite of the intensive felling and the high voltage cables and gas pipelines running across them, the Uglich forests still give hours of pleasure to mushroom-pickers, hunters and hikers."

SIGHTS

Shore excursions in Uglich tend to concentrate solely on the buildings in Uglich's old kremlin. The kremlin itself long ago lost its formidable appearance, and only traces of its stone walls can be seen. A section of an old moat survives, functioning today as a harbor for small boats.

Entering the kremlin and crossing the old moat, you approach the **Transfiguration Cathedral,** perched at the water's edge. Built in 1713, the green-domed cathedral is an active place of Orthodox worship, often resounding with song. The high vaulted ceiling unsupported by pillars creates a delicate interior drama and represents quite an engineering feat for its day. The splendid baroque iconostasis adds to the inspirational effect. Set off from the nave is an exhibition of valuable icons and religious artifacts through which local guides usually conduct a mildly interesting tour.

Outside, the cathedral's elegant belfry stands 37 meters high, crowned by a gilded dome recognizable from great distances. The Chaika watch factory installed an electronic bell with an hourly chime in the tower in 1984, but it seems to be broken quite often. You are not allowed to climb the bell tower, but you can enter the small antique shop located within.

The red **Church of St. Dmitry on the Blood,** perhaps the most fascinating edifice in the kremlin, stands nearby. Built in 1692 after the canonization of the murdered tsarevich Dmitry, the structure is a fine example of 17th century church architecture, designed with a love of embellishment, rich ornamentation and striking colors. Somewhat resembling a red-and-blue birthday cake owing to its ornate windows, decorative cornice, series of pilasters and star-studded cupolas, the church cannot help but enchant. Frescoes cover virtually all inner components, adding a dazzling presentation of color to the tight interior proportions. In the narthex-refectory, the portrayal of an unclothed Adam and Eve is an anomaly for Orthodox Church wall paintings. On the walls of the tiny nave the legend of the murder of Dmitry is rendered. The exiled bell of Uglich is also here. When Boris Godunov and his cronies were cleared of the murder of Dmitry, the ruling tribunal not only punished the townspeople of Uglich for having exacted retribution on the alleged assailants, but it also sentenced the bell that had rung out to alert the town of the crime. The bell was lashed, deprived of its tongue and one ear and exiled to Siberia. It seems happier now that it's back home. In front of the iconostasis lies the final element in the story of the murdered tsarevich: the litter on which the boy's exhumed corpse was carried to Moscow to prove that Dmitry was indeed deceased, thus precluding the appearance of any more False Dmitrys.

Another stop on the kremlin tour, the **Palace Chamber,** is a surviving section of the original palace complex built by Prince Andrey the Big in the 15th century. Altered and added to several times since its founding, the structure is a peculiar hybrid of original medieval architecture and curious subsequent additions. One of the oldest civic structures in this part of Russia, it now houses a museum of local antiquities, containing ho-hum displays of fabrics, tiles and other applied arts.

THE INSIDE SCOOP

The **walking tour of the kremlin**—the main activity of the stop—is worthwhile. You can do it by yourself, but you will miss out on all the information and possibly a short performance by a local choir. Groups will usually shy away from the green-domed Transfiguration Cathedral if an Orthodox service is being held inside, but individuals are free to break away and observe the service on their own (women should cover their heads, and men should not wear shorts).

Ships tend to spend very little time docked at Uglich. Usually you have just enough time to tour the kremlin, buy a few souvenirs and get back on board before departure. Should you have extra time, you might hire a paddleboat and wade around the Uglich Reservoir. The rental boatyard is located right off the embankment promenade on your way to town. All you need is your passport for a deposit and about a dollar for an hour's rental. Take your camera, as this is an opportunity to photograph the Uglich churches from an unbeatable, close-up perspective.

WHAT TO BUY IN UGLICH

Antiques. The small shop in the Transfiguration Cathedral's belfry is a good place to pick up genuine artifacts including samovars, jewelry, glass pharmacy jars, icons and tsarist rubles. Make sure you receive the necessary export documents if you acquire any valuable items. The main downtown souvenir shop offers antique items as well as the more predictable assortment of keepsakes.

Chaika watches. The Seagull brand of timepieces is indigenous to Uglich and is always a tourist obsession—rightly so, as Chaikas fetch up to $200 in the States, while here you can pick one up for one-tenth that price. These days you don't have to look very hard to find them; you will pass through a gauntlet of stands selling watches on your way to the kremlin. There is a also a factory outlet shop on the main downtown street with a catalogue of Chaikas for you to peruse. The rugged Soviet military watches are also found in Uglich and make good gifts for grandsons.

Cheese and sundries. Famous Uglich cheese is processed on the outskirts of town; but honestly speaking, there is no reason for it to be famous. You be the judge, and pick some up in one of the small food shops along the streets across from the kremlin. These shops are also great for picking up necessities for your cabin such as Russian chocolate and Armenian cognac.

WHERE TO EAT IN UGLICH

Along the embankment. Don't be shy about engaging the *babushkas* selling flowers and other home-grown treats along the quay. For pocket change you can pick up jars of fresh berries, bags of pickled cucumbers, nuts and other snacks. This is the main source of income for these ladies, so you might give your haggling instinct a rest.

Stariy Gorod Café. With a good location, at the end of the riverbank promenade as you walk towards the town from the ship, and tables outside and inside, the "Old Town" café is an easy place to stop for a quick drink and a snack before saying farewell to Uglich.

Uspenskaya Hotel (on the main square across from the kremlin). The café adjoining this recently opened hotel serves cheap mugs of Baltika beer and a full menu of snacks. Emphatically attesting to Russia's 21st century obsession with sushi, a wide selection can even be found here in Uglich—allegedly prepared by a Japanese chef!

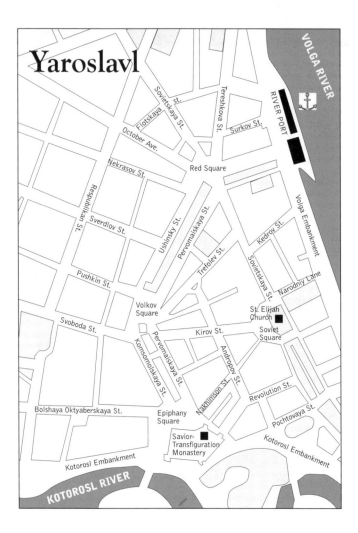

YAROSLAVL

ORIENTATION

Yaroslavl is among the oldest and most well known of all Russian provincial cities. A prosperous mercantile center in the past, it boasts a plethora of dazzling merchant churches and a lovely riverfront aspect.

HISTORY

In the 10th century, Finno-Ugric tribes occupied the towering banks above the Volga where the river is joined by a tributary, the Kotorosl River. Their outpost was called Bear Corner, as the pagan Finno-Ugrics revered and worshipped bears. Occasionally the tribes exploited their privileged riverfront position and ambushed passing merchant ships. Entreated by aggravated merchants, Rostov Prince Yaroslavl the Wise, along with some trusty men-at-arms, sailed past the settlement and successfully defended the merchants. Prince Yaroslavl then went ashore to talk the local inhabitants out of their pagan ways. The tribesmen responded by sicking a ferocious bear on the prince. In what must have been an impressive wrestling match, Prince Yaroslavl killed the bear, gaining the submission of the amazed onlookers. He ordered a church built and founded the city; the tribes were in no mood to argue. Thus goes the legend of the founding of ancient Yaroslavl in 1010.

In 1218 Yaroslavl became the capital of its own principality. It was sacked by the Mongol-Tatars in 1238 but remained an independent principality and important port for the next 225 years. Ivan the Great annexed the principality to Muscovy in 1463 during his surge for unification of the Russian lands. At the onset of the Time of Troubles in 1598, the Russian capital was transferred temporarily to Yaroslavl from imperiled Moscow. In 1612, with Moscow occupied by the Polish army, Russian heroes Minin and Pozharsky consolidated their citizens' army in Yaroslavl, going on to march on Moscow and evict the Poles. Cossack mercenaries lent a decisive hand during the battle, and the Time of Troubles was ended.

With order in the country restored and young Michael Romanov seated on the throne, the capital was moved back to Moscow in 1613. Yaroslavl suffered not. From 1613 to 1703 the city enjoyed a golden age, becoming the most prominent mercantile center of the upper Volga region. Trade routes from the Middle East and Europe converged on Yaroslavl, where merchants exchanged goods made of leather, silver, wood and exotic fabrics. One-sixth of Russia's wealthiest merchant families kept homes in Yaroslavl at this time; their neighbors were fellow traders from England or Holland.

The city's mercantile success spelled two things: churches and more churches. In order to stay in God's good graces (and also to one-up their southern neighbors in Moscow), wealthy merchant families sponsored the building of opulent religious edifices. By the end of the 17th century, no less than fifty new churches had been erected.

During the early 18th century Peter the Great saw to it that all attention focused on his new capital, St. Petersburg. Yaroslavl consequently fell from mercantile grace. The city persevered, though, developing industry and encouraging cultural growth. Russia's first national theater was founded in Yaroslavl in 1750, and the country's first major provincial newspaper was established here in 1786.

During the coming years industry continued to rear its head. By the middle of the 19th century, 12 textile plants and nearly seventy factories were steadily ejecting their fumes into the Volga air. A railroad to Moscow was laid in 1870, fostering more growth. All this industrial expansion, largely unregulated, nurtured worker discontent. As Soviet history relates, "The workers [of Yaroslavl] earned a mere pittance, went cold and hungry, and worked from sixteen to eighteen hours a day. Capitalist exploitation and lack of political rights led them to rise up against their oppressors." Textile workers organized a strike in 1895, and the 1917 Bolshevik Revolution was soon to follow.

After Yaroslavl was ruined by bloody post-revolution skirmishes between Red Guards and White Guards, the city settled obediently into its new Soviet role, which really didn't differ much from its old role. In the 1930s Yaroslavl factories turned out the Soviet Union's first heavy-duty trucks, trolley buses and diesel engines. The local rubber plant boasted of mass-producing the world's first synthetic rubber tires.

Today Yaroslavl's colorful ancient history and its comparatively muted recent history compete to define the city. An interesting indication of this is seen when reading street signs in Yaroslavl, many of which contain the current, Soviet-era street name as well as the pre-Soviet name. A recent Russian guidebook calls Yaroslavl "one of Russia's most polluted cities," yet the effects of industrial damage are not nearly as visible here as elsewhere farther down the Volga. The 70-year rule of the Soviets and their reckless push for progress resulted in the neglect and disappearance of many of Yaroslavl's famous churches, yet several of the city's most splendid structures survive.

ABOUT THE CITY

Connected to Moscow by all major transportation routes, including 280 kilometers of bandit-ridden highway, Yaroslavl remains an important commercial center. Most of the population of 650,000 are employed by local industries, including oil refining and manufacturing of rubber tires, diesel engines, textiles, enamels and paints. The city also is a livestock center, raising the renowned line of Romanovskaya sheep in addition to an allegedly distinctive breed of cattle. Perhaps having something to do with the distinctive cows, cheese from Yaroslavl is said to have been distinguished in international competitions.

SIGHTS

Although local sightseeing tours differ somewhat, brace yourself for a string of churches. The ones never missed are briefly described below.

A frequent warm-up stop is the red brick **Church of the Epiphany,** built in 1684-93. This striking building is known for its 17th century handcrafted glazed tiles adorning the exterior. Local craftsmen have actually replaced some of the original tiles with reproductions—see if you can distinguish the replacements from the authentics. Inside the church, frescoes painted in 1693 depict the life of Christ. A seven-tiered, gilded iconostasis rounds out the impressive interior.

The **Church of St. Elijah the Prophet** is a mainstay on the local tour itinerary and deservedly so. Built in 1647-50, the church features an asymmetrical exterior (created by five unevenly arranged green cupolas on the main building), covered galleries, a belfry, portico and bulky spire of an adjoining chapel. Frescoes painted in 1680 by renowned Kostroma artists blanket the entire interior. Nothing is left uncovered by the lively illustrative painting; the walls as well as the galleries, vaults, piers, window sills and portals are all graced with the artisans' original pigments. The church's lace-like iconostasis, undertaken in 1696, is regarded as a masterpiece of Russian baroque. The 1660 carved wooden thrones for the tsar and patriarch are also superb examples of the crafts of antiquity.

If the paved expanse (Ilyinskaya Square) engulfing the St. Elijah Church seems a bit too expansive, it is because Catherine the Great was so impressed with the church that she ordered all surrounding dwellings cleared away to maximize the structure's visibility. You can bet the Skripkin merchant family, whose home was ordered moved, were a bit miffed, as they paid for the church's construction. While standing in the square take note of the Soviet Executive Committee building (you'll know which one it is). It was designed to blend in with the square's earlier structures.

The main sightseeing destination in Yaroslavl is the **Savior-Transfiguration Monastery**. Founded in the 12th century, the monastery is one of the Volga's oldest and a regional sentimental favorite. Halfhearted restoration, indicated by perpetually vacant scaffolding, has been under way for as long as any local guide can remember. The gold-domed Transfiguration Cathedral, subsidiary chapels, main belfry, monks' cells and three-meter-thick fortress walls were all undertaken at various times during the 16th and 17th centuries. Imagine soldiers atop the fortress walls pouring boiling oil on their attackers in the midst of battle—it really happened here. In fact, the army that liberated Moscow during the Time of Troubles was assembled in Yaroslavl precisely because foreign invaders could not penetrate the monastery.

An area of the city not mentioned during shore excursions beyond a few introductory words is Yaroslavl's **embankment,** one of the most pleasant to be found among all Volga towns. The embankment, land-scaped in the mid-19th century, comprises a long promenade bordered by a picturesque greenbelt referred to as linden alley. The colonnaded gazebos, perched atop the bank, afford wonderful Volga panoramas. Should you opt to stroll along the promenade instead of exploring his-torical monuments, beware—two historic churches stand on the quay. The St. Elijah and St. Tikhon Church, built in 1830, is regarded as a masterpiece of Russian classicism. The structure, however, is in disrepair and may not be open to visitors. Hidden in a nearby courtyard, the St. Nicholas Nadeina Church (1649) is usually tended by a *babushka* who charges a nominal entrance fee. The interior frescoes are in bad shape, yet the overall setting somehow produces an alluring atmosphere.

THE INSIDE SCOOP

Yaroslavl has more remarkable medieval wall paintings than any other Russian town, so you owe it to yourself to go on the bus tour and check them out, even if you are growing weary of churches.

For logistical reasons the **Monastery Tour** cannot cover all the points of interest within the monastery walls, so you might have to venture off on your own to visit any that interest you. For example, groups don't climb the belfry, but the view from the top is breathtaking; there is no better point from which to photograph the city of Yaroslavl. A brown bear named Masha livess in a cage in the monastery and can be visited and photographed. There is also a natural history museum that will delight any enthusiast of taxidermy and which contains a special clock that maps the evolution of humankind onto a 24-hour period (at the moment, we are at 5:15 PM evolution time!). Admission to all these places must be purchased at the main entrance to the monastery.

Bus tours usually stop **downtown** amidst Yaroslavl's 18th century arcades for shopping. Nearby, the newly opened pedestrian zone, along Kirov Street, is the perfect place for the women to souvenir hunt while the men have a local beer at any of the many outdoor patios. You can even try your luck at an ATM in this part of town. If downtown is the last stop of the tour, don't be afraid to let the bus go back to the river terminal without you—it is an easy, ten-minute walk away. If you get lost, do what a Russian would do: stop the first passerby you see and ask, "*Gdye Volga?*" (Where's the Volga?).

Yaroslavl offers a rare opportunity of the journey: **Internet access.** Located on Nakhimson Street between the monastery and the Church of St. Elijah is Net Zone, a comfortable 24-hour Internet café with fifty terminals. The ruble equivalent of about $1.50 buys you an hour. Try to keep quiet about this, as it rather upsets ground excursions to have 250 passengers clammering to go to an Internet café.

If you still don't understand why Russian poet Apolon Grigoriev wrote, "The beauty of Yaroslavl cannot be described. Everywhere there is Volga, everywhere there is history," then it might be time to take a stroll along the **embankment promenade**. You might visit the two private museums located along the embankment: the enchanting Museum of Time and Music, which is the former home of a German composer who dabbled in watchmaking (or vice-versa), and the adjacent Museum of One Picture, whose name alone should suffice to draw you inside. Admission to each costs approximately one dollar.

WHAT TO BUY IN YAROSLAVL

Beer. The Yarpivo brand of beer is made locally and is available at many of the tents and patios around town. You should be able to find the bottled version inside any small market.

Clothing, cosmetics. There is no standout keepsake native to Yaroslavl, but this is one of the only stops, aside from Moscow and Petersburg, where you can check out the more traditional shopping scene. In the pedestrian zone (at Kirov Street 9/7) is the Womens' World department store, where you can find out what is popular with local Yaroslavl ladies.

Kvas. This is a uniquely Russian beverage made by fermenting black bread. It resembles beer but is not alcoholic. It was given to workers in Soviet times by the truckload to keep them toiling away towards a greater tomorrow. Today, you can sample a glass for a few rubles at small stands around Yaroslavl. Look for street vendors whose stands have a little keg on them bearing the word for *kvas* (КВАС). If you really like it, you are allowed to have a water bottle or even a pail filled with the stuff for you to take back to the ship.

WHERE TO EAT IN YAROSLAVL

Astoria (on Andropov Street). This complex offers a continental restaurant, a Japanese restaurant with sushi bar and a casino. A currency exchange is on the premises, so live it up.

Kirov Street. This recently opened pedestrian street is littered with cafés serving local beers and snacks. The Bristol Restaurant, on the second floor where Kirov Street meets Andropov Street, is a fine choice for a more prolonged meal, while Mario Pizza, across the street, is good for a quick fix of the pie.

Shato (Trefolev Street 20a). What they mean is "Chateau," and what they try to do in this romantic little restaurant is create just that kind of atmosphere.

Spasskiye Chambers (inside the Savior Transfiguration Monastery). Pull off your own coup in Russia and get a table for lunch or dinner at this exclusive restaurant located right in the Uglich Tower of the Savior-Transfiguration Monastery. First-rate Russian cuisine in a one-of-a-kind environment.

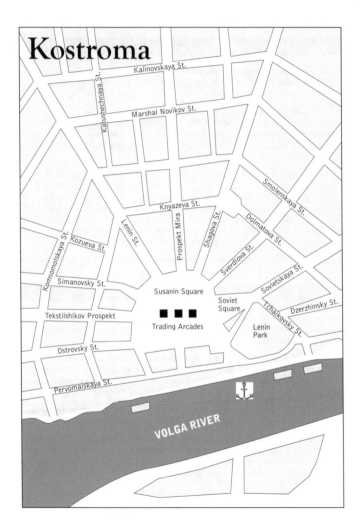

A VOLGA RIVER "RAKETA"

DOWNTOWN YAROSLAVL FROM THE SAVIOR-TRANSFIGURATION MONASTERY

KOSTROMA'S BELOVED IPATIEVSKY MONASTERY

BOYS OF KOSTROMA

KOSTROMA

ORIENTATION

Regarded as preserving the feel of typical Russian provinces, Kostroma is often used as the setting for Russian films and literature. Kostroma is also famous for its Ipatievsky Monastery, where the first tsar of the Romanov dynasty accepted the throne.

HISTORY

First mentioned in the Chronicles in 1237, Kostroma was founded somewhat earlier than that by pagan Slavs. Kostroma (pronounced kah-straw-má) was the name of a pagan god. On their way to sacking Yaroslavl in 1238, Mongol-Tatars first stopped in Kostroma for a dress rehearsal. By the mid-13th century the town had recovered and was an important port, belonging to the Vladimir principality.

In the 17th century the Time of Troubles officially ended when young Michael Romanov accepted the Russian throne from his place of hiding in Kostroma's Ipatievsky Monastery. With order re-established, Kostroma flourished alongside Yaroslavl, becoming the country's third most important city. During this period the city prospered on trade and boasted some of the country's finest fresco painters, who often were summoned to Yaroslavl to beautify the many churches being built there.

Like Yaroslavl, Kostroma saw its significance dwindle upon the founding of Russia's new capital, St. Petersburg. The town turned from mercantilism to manufacturing, although never entirely surrendering its role as an important Volga port. In 1773 a major fire devoured most of Kostroma. The city center was built anew, and by the end of the 18th century Kostroma had not only recovered but had established itself as a growing manufacturer of flax. By the turn of the century the city was known as the flax capital, supplying Russia and Europe with the very finest cloth with which to fabricate sails.

The city's glory days were long gone by the beginning of the 20th century. Kostroma plodded along, suffering many of the same woes as its Volga neighbors: unregulated industrial expansion, economic polarization, political oppression. A 1903 visitor satirically described the city thus: "The abundance of greenery, welcoming houses, and broad streets would create a rather attractive appearance were it not for the dust of the dry season and the mud of the rainy season. The sanitary state of the town cannot be envied, and the climate of Kostroma isn't very healthy. There is nearly no movement in the streets, and only during the navigation and on days of church processions (which occur about 100 times a year) does the town show signs of life."

The bulk of Kostroma's 20th century history reads more or less like that of Yaroslavl: declaration of Soviet power, Civil War destruction, nationalization of industrial and agricultural enterprises, razing of churches, economic stagnation.

ABOUT THE CITY

Russian sources describe the Kostroma region as historically possessing a "peculiar peasantry." The men were known to be tall, handsome, good-spirited and worldly because they often traveled to distant regions to peddle their wares. Because of the frequent absence of men, the women were considered more resourceful than most. Evidence of this characteriztion may not be readily apprehended by the passing visitor (or by anyone else, for that matter), but it provides an amusing perspective from which to view Kostroma's modern-day citizenry.

The present population of 300,000 is engaged in a variety of enterprises, including Kostroma's historical endeavor of processing flax, 60 percent of which is exported abroad after the raw material is imported from the very countries—Holland, Belgium and China among them—to which the finished product is exported. Like other historic Volga towns, Kostroma is a popular tourist destination, hosting 650,000 visitors annually.

SIGHTS

A staple on the Kostroma tour is a stop in the 18th century **city center.**
Local guides are extremely fond of pointing out that Kostroma is one
of the only Russian towns to preserve its original city center layout.
It's a dubious statement, for the city center was conceived by a pair of
St. Petersburg architects put in charge of *redesigning* it after a great fire
destroyed the original one in 1773. Original or not, the fanlike center
possesses peculiar charm and more trading arcades than almost any other
Russian town. Formerly the arcades had separate designations—flour
arcade, fish arcade, butter arcade—but today are either vacant or occupied by something a little strange, like an electronics shop or an ice
cream parlor.

Across the Kostroma River, approximately six kilometers from the
city center, stand the formidable white walls of the **Ipatievsky Monastery,** with the glittering golden cupolas of its cathedral hovering in
the background. A Tatar prince named Chet, a Godunov ancestor,
converted to Christianity and founded the Ipatievsky Monastery in 1332.
The Godunovs subsequently adopted the monastery as their personal
holy place, donating large sums of money for its continued growth and
improvement.

During Boris Godunov's reign (1598-1605), the monastery became
the country's wealth·iest. Boris's death did not spell the end of the
monastery's prosperity. On the contrary, it set in motion a chain of
events that ultimately made the monastery one of the most significant
in Russian history. Boris's death brought on the Time of Troubles, during which a young boyar named Michael Romanov, a distant relation
of Boris, took refuge in the monastery. Once the Poles were cleared out
of Moscow, an assembly of the land, consisting of Cossacks, Church
officials and military leaders, chose Michael to be the next tsar.

At first, Michael refused to accept the throne, probably fearing the
daunting scope and omnipresent perils of the job. But on 4 March 1613
the Ipatievsky Monastery stood surrounded by the entire population of
Kostroma anticipating an acceptance. Inside the compound were boyars,

military commanders, Moscow ambassadors, bishops, the Holy Patriarch of Russia and anyone else of high political station, all there to hail the ascension of the new tsar. Yet the young man of seventeen remained unswayed by the grandiose speeches and heartfelt imploorements, purportedly whimpering with internal strife throughout. Eventually so many people got on their knees that Michael had to consent. The church bells tolled and the crowd commenced singing. A new dynasty was born.

The Romanov family remained indebted to the monastery, adding to its wealth throughout their reign. By the end of the 17th century the monastery owned 22,000 hectares of land and 17,000 serfs. It was also a regional cultural center, housing a library of rare books and manuscripts. When an explosion in 1649 destroyed the monastery's Trinity Cathedral, built in stone by the Godunovs in 1590 to replace an original 14th century wooden church, the Romanovs promptly had it rebuilt. The austere, gold-domed structure made of white stone is still the focal point of the monastery. Inside the cathedral 17th century frescoes rendered by renowned Kostroma painters cover the walls. The graves of most of the Godunov family are housed here also.

The Soviets turned the Ipatievsky Monastery into the Kostroma Museum of History and Architecture, a comparatively sterile designation but one that at least enabled the monastery's preservation. Today, it is back in the hands of the Orthodox Church.

The **Museum of Wooden Architecture** is located in a serene setting adjacent to the monastery's walls. This is a favorite tourist destination, although not included in all ground excursions. Here amidst picturesque streams and woods stands a variety of handcrafted wooden structures from around the Kostroma region. Small churches, barns, windmills, boathouses and a series of peasant dwellings ranging from the modest to the opulent are open for your inspection.

On the way to or from the Ipatievsky Monastery, the bus may stop at the **Epiphany-Anastasia Convent,** a working convent that is home to some fifty nuns. As the main cathedral is an active place of worship, there likely won't be much of a tour here but rather free time to walk around and perhaps light a candle. Across the street from the entrance to the convent is the Kostroma municipal registry, where couples go on their wedding day to pick up their marriage license, so keep your eyes out for young brides, who generally love being photographed.

THE INSIDE SCOOP

The Ipatievsky Monastery is located several kilometers from the port across the Kostroma River, so you will want to take the bus there. The **Monastery Tour** covers some but not all of the points of interest inside the monastery, and the tour may not include a visit to the nearby Museum of Wooden Architecture. If you want to break away to visit anything not on the program, let your guide know you will be taking a taxi back to town.

Like that of Yaroslavl, the city center in Kostroma offers interesting shopping. Within the network of arcades, a farmers' market abounds with fruits and vegetables, while shops offer a range of antiques and other items. With a little time to meander, you can discover cheap draught beer, expensive cheeses, even thousand dollar Italian home appliances. The city center is only a five minute walk from the river terminal, so don't feel at the mercy of the tour bus for transport. Straying too far from the city center proper isn't exceptionally rewarding unless you have a penchant for exploring rundown provincial neighborhoods.

Kostroma's so-called flea market is located a few kilometers southeast of the city center, and occasionally a local guide may suggest visiting it. However, it is really nothing more than a crowded swap meet full of odds and ends, so you may want to choose to stay in town.

In contrast to Moscow, where the scene at the river port is desolate in comparison with downtown, here in Kostroma, if the weather is nice, the port area can be the liveliest spot in town, with outdoor cafés, activity on the river and a brand new promenade leading north along the Volga from the boat moorage. If you have time to spare and don't want to stray too far from the ship, taking a stoll along the promenade is a great way to see a slice of Kostroma in action.

WHAT TO BUY IN KOSTROMA

Kvas. As in Yaroslavl, you can sample a glass of this unique Russian non-alcoholic beverage at various places around the city. Here, in Kostroma, they tend to dispense *kvas* more traditionally, which is to say from industrial-looking yellow tanks that look like they should be holding hazardous chemicals. Look for one on the main square.

Linens. As you know from your tour, flax is the name of the game in Kostroma, whose history is intertwined (pardon the pun) with the production of flax sails. These days it may prove difficult to procure a genuine Kostroma spinnaker for your yacht back home, but you can pick up tablecloths, runners, napkins, shawls and the like. In front of the Ipatievksy Monastery are long rows of stalls selling linen. If you run out of time there, don't despair, more vendors await you back at the dock.

WHERE TO EAT IN KOSTROMA

Camelot (in the arcades along the main square). This is one of several cafés situated in the downtown arcades. This particular café always seems shady in more ways than one, which makes having a beer, coffee or snack here a fun experience.

PDK (on Sovietskaya Street just past Gornaya Street). This very pleasant café with an outdoor patio and cellar dining room specializes in pizza and other Italian dishes. Believe it or not, this is (gasp) a no-smoking establishment.

White Sun (at the rivership moorage). Named after the most famous Soviet-era movie, *White Sun of the Desert,* which was set in the Far East, this is not only the most convenient place to eat in Kostroma for a rivership passenger, but doubtlessly the most interesting, with delicious eastern cuisine, belly dancing and even hookahs. Lunch on weekdays only. Evenings, especially on weekends, book up fast.

GORITSY

ORIENTATION

Welcome to Goritsy (pop. 700), home to the Resurrection Convent, standing at the shoreline. From Goritsy a bus transports you to the town of Kirillov (pop. 8,000), eight kilometers away, to tour one of Russia's most famous monasteries, the Monastery of St. Kirill of the White Lake. Although most shore excursions concentrate solely on Kirillov, descriptions of both Kirillov and Goritsy follow.

Kirillov: Monastery of St. Kirill of the White Lake

At the very end of the 14th century an unusually pious monk named Kirill was appointed archimandrite (abbot) of Moscow's St. Simeon Monastery. But the 60-year-old man, fed up with the lack of spirituality he saw around him and feeling at the twilight of his life, abandoned his post to "wander around the Russian lands, bow to them, and find a remote region in which to live, as God shall show."

Kirill was thereafter spotted digging a cave atop a point at Lake Siverskoye's edge called Ivanovskaya Hill. By the following year the spry monk had erected two small churches, a cell for himself and quarters for those who might want to join him. Word spread about the holy old man on the hill, and pilgrims joined the recluse monk. Kirill welcomed all, so long as they adopted his ascetic ways. Monks at the monastery were said to live 100 years on average, owing to frequent fasting, subsisting in cold cells and taking herbs—very potent herbs, one would imagine.

The remote monastic haven expanded into an influential, landowning establishment. His personal asceticism notwithstanding, Kirill constantly sought to enrich the monastery's holdings. He did so by allowing the monastery to serve as a northern bulwark for the Muscovy princedom, thereby gaining endowments as well as political influence. By the time of his death, 30 years after arriving here, Father Superior

Kirill had established the monastery not only as a home for disciplined religious worship, but as a feudal lordship administrating a host of villages and forty separate plots of land.

Kirill's program of religious regimentalism and political adroitness was followed by his successors. Father Superior Trifon in 1433 did some favors for Grand Prince Vasily II and won funds that helped erect the Assumption Cathedral in 1497. Vasily II's son, Ivan the Great, continued to extend to the monastery great privileges, including free trading rows in Moscow and tax-exempt status on earnings. Ivan the Great's son Vasily III sponsored the construction of two more cathedrals: the Archangel Gabriel Cathedral and the Church of St. John the Precursor. The gesture was in gratitude for the result of a desperate visit he and his infertile wife made to the monastery to pray for an heir. Their prayers were answered in the form of a son, the future Ivan the Terrible.

Tsar Ivan, feeling indebted to the monastery for the miracle of his own birth, continued to lavish it with gifts, donating silver, precious stones, vestments and rubles to its ever-growing booty. Much of the money went toward fortifying the monastery with stone walls, parts of which still stand today. Ivan also began using the monastery as a place of exile, to which he sent adversarial boyars, princes and even priests. It is also said that at the end of his life, suffering from howling madness, Ivan submitted to the monastery a confession containing the names of thousands of people he had ordered killed during his reign.

The monastery remained loyal to Moscow throughout the Time of Troubles, defending against foreign invaders. Michael Romanov, who emerged from the political tumult to accept the Russian throne, naturally was appreciative of the monastery's service and donated more money. The beginning of the Romanov dynasty also signaled a change in the monastery's role from country club for exiles to genuine prison for convicted criminals. Russia's Holy Patriarch Nikon was locked up here after being stripped of his title for being too fanatical. The cell he inhabited afforded a view of a church whose architecture he particularly loathed.

In the middle of the 18th century the monastery reached the apex

VILLAGERS OF IRMA

VOLOGDA PRODUCE

MONASTERY OF ST. KIRILL IN KIRILLOV

LOCK OF THE VOLGA-BALTIC CANAL

of its prosperity, with holdings consisting of 20,000 serfs, 400 villages, a salt works and God only knew how much cash.

Descent from the apex later followed. Greed, mismanagement and moral corruption set in motion the monastery's decline. While political exiles continued to arrive throughout the 18th century and well into the 19th, the fortress itself, no longer of military utility, suffered neglect. The brotherhood began hawking fortifications and armory, and the tower chambers were rented out to store salt and vodka. Of the spiritual environment within the monastery at this time, a visitor wrote, "There are no morals, no piety, no cares about anybody or anything. The archimandrite never takes his meals at the refectory, the vice-regent has been on a bender for two months, and the 'brothers'—if they didn't get dead drunk in my face it was only because of a shortage [of spirits]." The pinnacle of the decline came after Tsar Alexander II freed the serfs in 1861, causing the archimandrite and brotherhood to sell on the black market some 4,000 valuable manuscripts to remain financially soluble.

During the Civil War that followed the 1917 Revolution the monastery sided with the White Guards in hopes of defeating the atheistic Bolsheviks. When the counter-revolution failed, the Bolsheviks shot the monastery's reigning bishop along with other conspirators. The new government placed the monastery under state control in 1923, calling it a museum of local studies.

In 1969 the Soviet government declared the monastery a historical and architectural museum, ensuring its continuous albeit lackluster restoration. Since *perestroika,* many churches and monasteries have been returned to the Church, but owing to the sheer size of the monastery and the scope of renovation, the archbishop decided it best not to push too hard for the immediate return of this particular piece of pious property.

So although still officially a museum, there is a small "operating part" of the monastery, which is rented from the government on a 150-year lease and headed by two monks and a staff of a dozen helpers, including gardeners, carpenters, cooks, etc.—all of whom are on Church salary to keep Kirill's dream alive.

Goritsy: Resurrection Convent

The Resurrection Convent was founded in 1544 by Moscow Princess Ye-frosiniya, wife of Ivan the Great's youngest son, Prince Andrey Staritsky. Yefrosiniya was among a group of boyars who opposed the reigning tsar, Ivan the Terrible, and were plotting to assassinate him and install on the throne Yefrosiniya's son Vladimir. In 1563 Ivan the Terrible uncovered the plot, and heads started to roll. Yefrosiniya was exiled to the very convent she founded in Goritsy.

With an inkling that her exile might be lengthy, Yefrosiniya arrived with her servants and embroidery workshop in tow. (Some of the palls she sewed are exhibited in the monastery in Kirillov.) She quickly tired of monastic life, though, and began appealing regularly to Ivan the Terrible for her pardon and release. The tsar, fed up with the constant pleas, one day sent word to the convent that Yefrosiniya was to be freed. He sent to Goritsy a ship, which collected the princess, promptly took her to the middle of the Sheksna River, and drowned her.

Yefrosiniya was the first in a long line of women exiled to the convent. Ivan the Terrible, satisfied that the convent rid him of one troublesome relation, exiled his fourth wife here as well. The convent regularly hosted 50 to 500 exiled women in addition to its regular sisterhood.

Structures in the convent include three churches: the Resurrection Cathedral, the early 17th century St. Dmitry Chapel and belfry and the early 19th century Trinity Cathedral. Unfortunately, the convent has been in a dilapidated state since Soviet times. In 1997 a restoration program began, but aside from an occasional fresh coat of paint on the riverside walls, there is not much evidence of progress.

THE INSIDE SCOOP

You would be ill-advised to bypass the excursion to Kirillov, as the Monastery of St. Kirill of the White Lake is the main attraction of this stop. The **Monastery Tour** presents you with icon-o-rama, but actually this is a very good time and place to learn about icons if you haven't already. Exhibitions inside the monastery also provide an excellent opportunity to scrutinize local handicrafts, including superb examples of famous

Vologda lace. You generally don't have time to go off and explore the town of Kirillov itself; don't fret, you're not missing anything.

Back in Goritsy after the tour, you may have free time before embarkation. You are certainly free to walk over to the Resurrection Convent for a little adventure, or for another kind of experience, walk up the main road and see if you meet any locals. A sure bet awaits you just a few houses up the road at number 26, an unmistakable wooden dwelling covered with decorative carvings and a sign reading "Welcome to Our House." Don't be shy, go on in and meet the proprietor.

WHAT TO BUY IN GORITSY/KIRILLOV

Any of these items are easily procured at the stalls or in the small shops at the dock in Goritsy.

Ceramics and woodcrafts. Vologda handiwork also includes painted ceramics such as tea sets or miniatures, as well as figurines and baskets made of woven and sometime painted birch.

Foodstuffs. The Kirillov area is proud of producing breads and biscuits, butter, sausages and smoked fish. Should you see any of these items, they likely will be locally produced and fresh.

Fortified wine. Not far from the monastery in Kirillov is a winery that produces fortified wines made of local fruits such as currants and cranberries. Several of the small shops in Goritsy will even offer you a tasting before you buy.

Vologda lace. You are in the heart of Vologda, a region known for its famous lace, which has been distinguished in world fairs of the early 20th century and elsewhere. The lace is known to be delicate and intricate yet strong and weighty. It is usually made from flax, cotton or sometimes silk. Shawls, scarves, dresses, cuffs, collars and doilies are representative pieces of this handicraft.

WHERE TO EAT IN GORITSY/KIRILLOV

There's not much choice here. The only chance for a snack is near the dock in Goritsy. Usually a few locals run a barbecue on the lawn. Here you can sample traditional Russian *shashlik* (shish kabob) and regional beer. Local *babushkas* also tend to make their way down to the pier when a big ship is docked. They offer cups of berries, small home-baked pies, jams, pickles and the like.

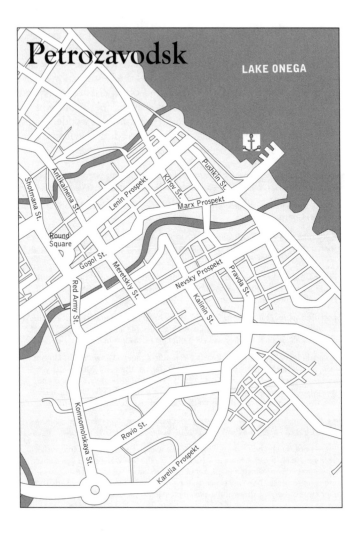

PETROZAVODSK

ORIENTATION
Petrozavodsk, located fifty-five kilometers across Lake Onega from Kizhi Island, is the capital of the Karelian Republic. It is a clean yet nondescript city whose claims to fame are its origin as an armory foundry, a superb native dance troupe called Kantele and a Ben and Jerry's ice cream parlor. Some ships call on Petrozavodsk on their way to/from famous Kizhi Island, while otherS bypass the city altogether.

HISTORY
Petrozavodsk stands on the site of a 17th century settlement called Olonets. With the Northern War against Sweden getting under way in 1700, Peter the Great ordered the settlement to establish iron foundries and armament workshops to supply the military with cannons, cannonballs and assorted weaponry. The first blast furnace of the Petrovsky Foundry was erected in 1703, and a month later the first naval cannon was cast. Over one hundred top armorers were sent to the plant from the Kremlin Armory Chamber in Moscow to assist in the production of war necessities such as cannons, pistols, muskets and swords, in addition to war luxuries like gilded copper cutlass hilts, monogrammed powder horns and gilded silver and copper belt buckles. Demonstrating unsettling versatility, the armory in its spare time turned out medical instruments.

Thirteen years after the official defeat of Sweden in 1721, the Petrovsky Foundry closed. Catherine the Great reopened it in 1772 to supply weapons to her Turkish military campaign. In 1777, with Turkish submission achieved, Catherine renamed the works Alexandrovsky in honor of the birth of her grandson, future Emperor Alexander I. The settlement that had grown around the ironworks was renamed *Petrozavodsk*, meaning "Peter's factory-town." Eight years later Petrozavodsk became the capital of the Olonets region, presided over by the city's first mayor, an acclaimed Russian poet named G.R. Derzhavin.

In the 19th century activity in Petrozavodsk began to wane because of the lack of railway connections to major centers. With wooden houses lining the streets and outdated metallurgy equipment laboring in the Alexandrovsky works, the city assumed a new function as tsarist exile. Thus another acclaimed poet, Fyodor Glinka, who participated in the 1825 Decembrists' demonstration in St. Petersburg, was installed in Petrozavodsk. Glinka's exile here lasted until 1830.

By the beginning of the 20th century Petrozavodsk was well stocked with political exiles. Bolshevik agitators took root in the Alexandrovsky Ironworks in September 1917, and Soviet power was proclaimed in the city the following year. In 1923 Petrozavodsk was named capital of the newly formed Karelian Republic. The Soviet government converted Petrozavodsk's armaments plants into manufacturers of construction equipment for large-scale civil engineering projects. By 1940 the city had been turned into a Soviet economic and cultural center, featuring 46 major industrial enterprises and a host of educational and research institutes.

At the onset of World War II Petrozavodsk transported practically its entire manufacturing operations to a safer but colder region in Siberia. The move turned out to be shrewd, as by the end of the war the Soviets had bombed away most of the city trying to force out the Finnish troops who had invaded in an attempt to regain eastern Karelia for Finland. With 60 percent of its buildings destroyed, the city resigned itself to a long period of reconstruction after liberation finally was had on 28 June 1944. From the end of the war until the recent dissolution of the Soviet government in 1991, Petrozavodsk lumbered along as the so-called economic and cultural center it was designed to be. Not much has changed since then, but on a nice day Petrozavodsk offers fine strolling, shopping and eating.

ABOUT THE CITY

Privileged with a sprawling lakefront aspect, the city of 250,000 people nonetheless is concentrated inland. Typical of the north, the climate is severe, with winters pre-empting autumns and lasting until April. June white nights bring twenty hours of sunshine per day as well as warmer temperatures, which peak in July. The population is predominantly employed by various local industries, including mica and lumber processing, furniture and footwear production, prefabricated home construction and fish canning. The city's mainstay is still metalworking. A rather anomalous enterprise located here is a Ben and Jerry's ice cream manufacturer. The company originally set its sights on Moscow, but because Moscow's taxes were too high, it quite happily came to Petrozavodsk.

Although local sources mention 40 different nationalities represented in the city, one would be hard-pressed to find anyone but Russians, who comprise ninety percent of the population, with Karelians and Finns dividing the remaining ten percent. Nevertheless, the city is considered the heart of Finnish culture in Russia. Residents of Petrozavodsk decided not to take down their Communist-era monuments or to reinstate pre-Revolutionary street names. The predominant sentiment is that the past cannot and should not be erased by making mere cosmetic changes.

SIGHTS

The park near the river terminal is really the only surviving part of the original settlement, as Catherine the Great was so impressed with it that she decreed it a preserve area. If the statue of Peter the Great seems a little out of place tucked back into the trees here on the city's outskirts, it's because it was moved here from its original prominent location in Round Square to make way for—who else?—Lenin.

Kirov Square is the first main square encountered from the river terminal. It is the former site of the Peter and Paul Cathedral, a wooden structure built for Peter the Great in 1703 and long since toppled. Now the predominant feature is metal structures resembling scaffolding planted into the sidewalks bordering the square. These supports formerly displayed Communist Party banners bearing bewildering slogans such as "The Party is the Avant-Garde of the Working Class!" Now they carry advertisements for cigarettes and lotteries.

Farther along the main street (Marx Prospekt) the curiosities continue with a 1960 statue of Marx and Engels sitting on a bench and having a little chat (guess what about). Still farther, opposite the town department store, lies the center of the long city park, "laid out in the 1930s by local residents in their spare time to make Petrozavodsk a green city," according to local literature.

Marx Prospekt culminates in Round Square, an oxymoronic name that might be interpreted as epitomizing tsarist as well as communist will toward natural order. Encircling the square (ensquaring the circle?) is a complex of former residences of the original management of the Alexandrovsky Ironworks. At the center of the square stands a granite statue of Lenin sculpted in typically imposing, inartistic socialist style. Where the square joins the city park lies the Tomb of the Unknown Soldier; the eternal flame was lit from that of a twin memorial in St. Petersburg's Mars Field.

Back near Kirov Square and across the Lososinka River lies the other side of Petrozavodsk, a more residential region through which tour buses quickly zoom. The Petrozavodsk Museum of Local Studies, in which fine examples of local iron craftsmanship are displayed, is located here. A few blocks away stands the blue-domed Exaltation of the Cross Cathedral, an active church set amongst overgrown trees. The adjacent cemetery, invaded by foliage, produces a somber yet compelling effect.

THE INSIDE SCOOP
The main reason to call on Petrozavodsk is that it is a convenient base from which to make an excursion to famed Kizhi Island. However, like virtually every stop along the route, Petrozavodsk affords river travelers a distinct experience. With a repertoire of only marginally interesting sights, the city instead offers an opportunity to glimpse typical Russian daily life. By strolling the two-kilometer length of Marx Prospekt, which commences at the base of the river terminal and culminates in Round

Square, you pass not only the majority of the sights listed above but a number of small shops and cafés within which the occasionally mystifying play of everyday Russian life is acted out.

Whether you stroll Marx Prospekt, cross the Lososinka River to visit the Exaltation of the Cross Cathedral, or explore an entirely different route, this is your chance to indulge in a little *nezateilivoye razvlecheniye*, or "modest fun." Have coffee and pastries in a small café; peruse the bizarre array of items in the town department store; or take care of small errands, as you won't be seeing real civilization for about two days after this, regardless of which direction your ship is heading.

Regarding Ben and Jerry's, some buses make a stop there, some don't. Usually it is decided by a show of hands on the bus. If your group votes to go eat ice cream and you would rather see sights, change buses. If you *are* craving a waffle cone fix, a bus is your best bet, as the parlor is a bit out of the way.

WHAT TO BUY IN PETROZAVODSK

Baskets, figurines, carvings. Karelia is known for its handicrafts made from the indigenous Karelian birch trees. Articles are often made of thin strips woven together or by carving larger blocks.

Embroidery. Made of cotton, wool or silk, embroidered items from Karelia date back as far as the 13th century and traditionally feature geometrical compositions.

WHERE TO EAT IN PETROZAVODSK

Business Club (behind the Intourist Hotel). Very good continental cuisine with an innocently racy cabaret show after dinner (weekends only).

Finnish Theater. The café and bar here can get very lively, especially on weekend nights.

Petrovsky (on Marx Prospekt right before Round Square). This Petrozavodsk mainstay serves excellent Russian and Karelian cuisine in the cellar of a former 18th century jail.

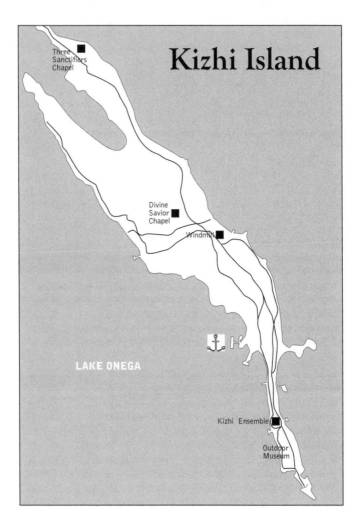

Kizhi Island

Three
Sanctifiers
Chapel

Divine
Savior
Chapel

Windmill

LAKE ONEGA

Kizhi Ensemble

Outdoor
Museum

KIZHI ISLAND

ORIENTATION
Situated in the northeast of Lake Onega, the island of Kizhi is home to a world famous outdoor museum-preserve featuring edifices of northern wooden architecture, including the remarkable Transfiguration Cathedral.

HISTORY
Accurate documentation of the history of Kizhi is scarce, largely because of the island's remoteness. The generally accepted version of its early beginnings is that it was an ancient pagan ritual site for northern tribes. Despite the presence of the pagans, Russian settlers established a parish on the island in the 11th century. The island became more populated as Russians fled Mongol-Tatar wrath in the south to the protected Novgorod principality in the north and as Novgorod serfs escaped to the east to seek an independent life. With an abundance of fish, game and fertile soil, the island and its surroundings continued to attract hardy settlers throughout the 12th and 13th centuries.

In 1478 Ivan the Great annexed Novgorod to Muscovy. With a fondness for centralizing territory that made him the father of Russian bureaucracy, Ivan began exacting taxes on the Kizhi *pogost*. By the next century the territory of Kizhi extended for 40 kilometers around the island and included 130 small villages. At this time thirteen villages and two churches stood on Kizhi itself.

During the Time of Troubles the *pogost* alternately was at the mercy of Poles, Lithuanians and Swedes, all of whom were poised to overrun the country. Kizhi villagers dispersed into the countryside. When they returned, they found themselves acting as border guards on an island-cum-defense-post, a role they relished not. When Peter the Great decided to put an end to the Swedish threat once and for all, he summoned peasants from Kizhi to work in his newly established armory plant in Petrozavodsk. For all practical purposes Russia had won the war by 1709, and the Transfiguration Cathedral was erected on Kizhi in 1714 partly in commemoration of the victory. The Intercession Church, built fifty years later, was the last symbol of flourishing on the island. As increasing numbers of craftsmen left Kizhi to work in St. Petersburg, the island entered a period of decline in the 19th century from which it never recovered.

One of the first acts of the Bolshevik government was to issue a conservation decree mandating that certain antique wooden buildings of the Onega region be preserved because they "represent the results of genuinely proletarian creativity, showing how during times of persecution and oppression our people were able to convincingly portray their beliefs, hopes, and aspirations." Its rhetoric aside, the decree saved the two extraordinary churches standing on Kizhi Island. Moreover, it resulted in the island's acquisition of examples of traditional architecture from around the Onega region. An outdoor museum was thus formed, opening in 1966, and in 2000 the Kizhi museum-preserve was placed on the UNESCO World Heritage List.

ABOUT THE ISLAND

Kizhi is small and narrow, measuring approximately six kilometers by one kilometer. Its northern location in Lake Onega makes for misty early mornings and dazzling dawns in summer. The most notorious creature on the island (besides the pesky mosquito) is the adder snake, or European viper, which is said to slither around in the long grass. Rarely is its bite fatal to humans, and even more rarely is one actually seen by a tourist. Locals, on the other hand, allow the creatures to come into their homes, as the ancient serpents are believed to indicate fields of the earth's kinetic energy, thereby instructing on the proper feng shui of the interior decor.

SIGHTS

Officially called the State Historical, Architectural and Ethnographic Preserve of Kizhi, the collection of structures planted predominantly along the southern tip of the island consists of churches, chapels, bell towers, peasant houses, granaries, barns, windmills and bathhouses—all brought from around the Onega region to illustrate the architecture common to the Russian north. The focal point, referred to as the Kizhi Ensemble, comprises the awe-inspiring Transfiguration Cathedral, the neighboring Intercession Church and the bell tower between the two. The two churches of the ensemble are the only structures originally built on the island.

Thirty thousand shingles on 22 separate cupolas situated on five tiers compose the ascending nest that is the **Transfiguration Cathedral,** built in 1714. It actually was built as a mere summer church and—as your guide will be sure to mention—entirely without nails. (The nails visible today are from restoration in the 1960s.) Popular legend has it that the cathedral was built by one man with only one tool, an ax. The interior, now closed to visitors, was beautified with a gilded iconostasis and hosted church services until 1937.

The shingles are made of aspen wood, which resists weathering fairly well, responds to aging very well and is capable of reflecting a myriad magical hues. Midday sunshine makes them shimmer like silver, while the light of dawn or dusk turns them into blazing gold. To avoid placing scaffolding on the famous tourist attraction, yearly maintenance and waterproofing of the shingles is performed by mountaineering specialists hanging on ropes.

In connection with the church's placement on the World Heritage List, in 2006 the most comprehensive restoration of the building to date commenced. Over an eight-year period, sections of the church (seven sections in all) will be dismantled in turn and taken to a workshop at the northern end of the island for restoration before being returned to their original place on the building. In this way, the program will have minimal impact on tourists' cameras. In 2014, the church, including the interior, will be opened anew in its best condition ever.

The interior of the nearby **Intercession Church** is open to visitors and houses icons from its closed neighbor. Built in 1764 as a winter church, its roof too was constructed without nails. Some historians argue that the structure was intended to support a gabled roof, but being left unfinished for a time, it was given a flat roof with nine shingled cupolas to better complement the Transfiguration Cathedral. Considering the church's irregular proportions, it's a plausible theory.

The 1874 **bell tower,** which until recently was open for climbing, completes the ensemble of fir, pine and aspen called by one observer "an original song in wood."

Other significant structures through and around which you will be dutifully conducted are the modest Chapel of the Resurrection of Lazarus (built in 1391, making it the oldest standing wooden church in Russia), the Chapel of the Archangel Michael (whose belfry bells are sometimes played by a local for your enjoyment) and a series of authentic peasant houses and farm structures.

When time permits, some guides will lead their group after the tour to the more pastoral central part of the island, where the small 18th century Divine Savior Chapel sits atop a hill from which you command a marvelous view on the island and the lake. On the way there, you will pass a windmill, built in 1921, and the island's cemetery, an overgrown hodge-podge of uniquely assembled grave sites that would strike envy into the heart of a modern-day mixed-media artist.

THE INSIDE SCOOP

This is a pretty straightforward scene. You're on a small island with a lot of different examples of ancient northern architecture and you have well-informed local guides (actually they boat over from Petrozavodsk) to show and tell you everything you ever wanted to know about the place.

If your tour did not include a walk to the northern part of the island and you have a minimum of an hour to spare, you are free to take in the refreshing Kizhi countryside on your own. Follow the trail away from the outdoor museum over some rolling hills and past the island's small cemetery to the windmill and fArther to the hilltop Divine Savior Chapel, where a truly divine view awaits. Those with even more time and energy (another 1.5 hours minimum) could continue to the northern end of Kizhi, past the 17th century Chapel of the Three Sanctifiers, to the very tip of the island, marked by an 1886 windmill overlooking the water.

Photographing the churches of Kizhi is always the main preoccupation of visitors. You may have heard this tip before, but because of the unique composition of the churches' shingles, nowhere is it more important than here: lighting is key. Watch the clouds very carefully and note the time of day of your visit. You can shoot 100 frames of the Transfiguration Cathedral from every angle while on the tour, but if the light is flat, so will be your results. A few moments of sunlight at either dawn or dusk can turn an otherwise blasé image of the Transfiguration Cathedral into a sparkling prizewinner.

WHAT TO BUY ON KIZHI

Cappuccino. A sole cappuccino vending machine is planted rather incongruously and certainly unexpectedly at the Kizhi dock. Why not give it a try?

Embroidery. Made of cotton, wool or silk, embroidered items from Karelia date back as far as the 13th century and traditionally feature geometrical compositions.

Weavings and jewelry. Often during the tour of the island you will be treated to an exhibition of local weaving or jewelry-making inside one of the houses. These handicrafts are made on the spot using traditional methods and generally are for sale. There is no more authentic keepsake from Kizhi, other than perhaps a viper bite.

WHERE TO EAT ON KIZHI

Kizhi Restaurant. Located at the dock, this floating restaurant with a view of the Kizhi ensemble in the distance is the only game in town on Kizhi, serving drinks and light meals daily from 08:00–21:00.

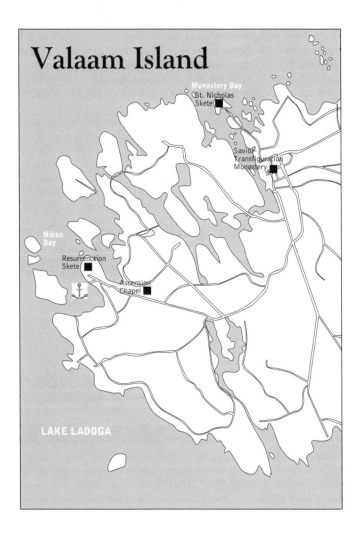

Valaam Island

Monastery Bay
St. Nicholas
Skete

Savior-
Transfiguration
Monastery

Nikon
Bay

Resurrection
Skete

Ascension
Chapel

LAKE LADOGA

THE "ENSEMBLE" OF KIZHI ISLAND

MANDROGI'S VODKA MUSEUM

THE LANDSCAPE OF VALAAM ISLAND

THE START OF THE SCHOOL YEAR ON VALAAM

VALAAM ISLAND

ORIENTATION
Valaam is the main island of a rugged archipelago tucked into northeastern Lake Ladoga. The island constitutes a unique and diverse northern natural preserve and is home to one of the Russian Orthodox Church's most sacred monasteries.

HISTORY
The story of Valaam is inextricably linked to the saga of its Transfiguration Monastery, the centerpiece of a necklace of religious edifices that at one time numbered 23 churches and 19 chapels adorning Valaam and the surrounding islands. Legend tells that two Greek monks, Herman and Sergius, founded the monastery in the year 992, thereby establishing the most northwest outpost of the Orthodox Church. When Herman and Sergius died, their remains defied decomposition, earning the monks canonization. Their monastery, however, was not as lucky and was completely destroyed in 1163.

The better documented and more believable version of the monastery's founding is that it sprung up in 1329 as a base for missionaries plying their trade in Karelia.

Although historians argue over whether or not the structure originally was fortified, they agree that the island was the sight of repeated confrontations between the Swedish kingdom and the Novgorod principality. Notwithstanding a period of relative flourishing from the mid-14th to the mid-15th century, the monastery was ravaged periodically by the Swedes until Peter the Great subdued them finally in the early 18th century. In 1715 Peter himself visited Valaam, ordering the restoration and protection of the monastery.

The island thereafter developed into a regional economic center with international spiritual influence. Valaam missionaries ventured as far as the Aleutian Islands and Alaska to seed Orthodox beliefs. In 1822 the monastery was bestowed with first class status, and a few decades later professional architects of the Russian Style school began restoring and adding to the monastery complex. Wealthy visitors from St. Petersburg, reaching the island on newly opened water routes in 1843, contributed to the revival. By the end of the century nine new *sketes*, or subsidiary colonies, had been constructed on and around the island. The monastery, at this time one of the wealthiest in the country, found itself at the head of its own mini-state, operating factories and developing agriculture.

During this period of revival Valaam also became a popular holiday destination. Visiting during summers, Orthodox pilgrims were joined by notable artists, writers and scientists seeking spiritual refreshment. Famous Russian painters Kuindzhi, Shishkin and Rerikh all spent time on the island, as did the composer Tchaikovsky, who recuperated here from a nervous breakdown inflicted by the pressure of writing his first symphony.

While visitors sought inspiration, monks inhabiting the outlying *sketes* observed a stoic regime, including prohibition on the presence of women. The prohibition was lifted, however, one day per year. (And what a day that likely was.) The monastic island lifestyle also attracted large numbers of *bogomoltsy*, a regiment of monks dedicated to praying for the sovereign.

In 1917, when Lenin and Trotsky summarily excused Russia from World War I, Valaam became the domain of Finland. The monastery continued to thrive. By 1938 the population of nearly 200 monks maintained a hostel, a candle manufactory, a forge, a complex of art studios and workshops and a shipyard. In addition, they engaged in fishing, agriculture and horticulture.

Two years later, in 1940, the monks found themselves scurrying en masse to mainland Finland when Stalin regained the island for the atheistic Soviet Union. In Finland the monks founded the New Valaamo Monastery to house the icons, vestments and 30,000-volume Slavonic library with which they wisely absconded. Rumor has it they even took the remains of the monastery's legendary founders, St. Herman and St. Sergius. Back on Valaam, the Soviets closed the Transfiguration Monastery, shooed away any remaining monks and opened a naval academy.

In keeping with the trend induced by *perestroika*, the government in 1989 returned several Valaam structures to the Orthodox Church. Soon thereafter the first six monks of a new era arrived on the island. In summer of 1992 President Boris Yeltsin was joined on the island by Holy Patriarch of Russia Alexiy II to sign a decree restoring the entire monastery complex to the Church.

ABOUT THE ISLAND

Occupying 36 square kilometers over Lake Ladoga's greatest depths of 230 meters, the Valaam archipelago consists of one main island and 50 smaller ones, all made up of granite and diabase. The largest island, Valaam, occupies 28 square kilometers. It is home to the greatest variety of flora, largely owing to the horticultural efforts of monks over the centuries. Coniferous forests cover much of the island, while alleys of fir and larch trees as well as groves of cedar, oak and apple trees stand amidst stretches of meadows. In all, over 460 varieties of plant life take root in the island.

Although wildlife enthusiasts would be lucky to spot the elk, fox, hare and ermine that inhabit the remoter areas, birdwatchers might catch sight of finches, siskins, thrushes and chiff-chaffs. From the shores, gulls and even seals can be seen. Valaam is a natural wildlife preserve, which means that nothing on the island should be killed—including the ubiquitous monster-size mosquitoes that relish tourist blood.

SIGHTS

The ship approaches Valaam from the southwest, hooking around a few small islands and then gliding into Nikon's Bay, named after the fanatical 17th century patriarch of Russia. Anchor is cast at the base of a hill upon which stands one of Valaam's small secluded mini-monasteries, the **Resurrection Skete.** The hill itself is called New Jerusalem, a tribute to one of the far-off destinations of pilgrimage to which Valaam monks have ventured. There is not a lot of action at this end of the island, with most restoration and religious activity being conducted at and around the main Transfiguration Cathedral, six kilometers away. Entertaining local tour guides usually make the most of your visit to the skete, however, also taking you for a short walk to the nearby Ascension Chapel of the Gethsemane Skete, also uninhabited.

A ferry trip to the **Transfiguration Monastery** is often offered as an optional tour. After gliding into Monastery Bay and docking, you disembark and approach the monastery by climbing 62 granite steps to an outlying yard. To the right of the footpath stands the tiny Tsar's Chapel, commemorating the visit of Alexander II in 1858. To the left stands an obelisk paying tribute to the visit of Peter the Great. The path leads through an archway known as the Holy Gates, the main entrance to the monastery. The arch supports the Church of Peter and Paul above, crowned by a single cupola.

The Transfiguration Cathedral, built in 1887 on the site of earlier cathedrals, is topped with five azure domes and adjoined by a 70-meter-high lighthouse-belfry containing a colossal sixteen ton bell that sounds the hour. Massive renovation from 1993-2003 has resulted in the transformation of the once decrepit split-level interior into a spectacular inner sanctuary covered with lively painting and gilded icons. Guides will tell you that this stupendous renovation was financed by private donations, but judging from the shiny Orthodox Church SUV often parked in the monestary courtyard, the Church lended more than a helping hand in getting the place back in shape.

THE INSIDE SCOOP
You would be ill-advised to miss the tour to the Transfiguration Monastery, as it really is the main attraction of the island, aside from the archipelego's striking natural beauty, of which you get the best view onboard the ferry ro the monastery.

It is also possible to walk to the monastery, join the tour there and take the ferry back. But do make sure you join the excursion at the monastery, or else you will have a hard time accessing the church interiors and may miss out on any special arrangements, such as a choir concert.

Give yourself a minimum of one hour to reach the monastery by foot. Simply follow the dirt road leading away from the dock until you see a road sign marking kilometer zero of your six-kilometer hike. You will see signs along the road every kilometer to mark your progress. The scenery is sublime, and the forests offer excellent berry and mushroom picking. Should you tire along the way, flag down the occasional car that comes along the road and ask for a lift.

WHAT TO BUY ON VALAAM

Only a few stands are set up at the ship moorage and near the entrance to the Transfiguration Monastery, offering the typical array of souvenirs.

Smoked fish and other homemade delicacies. At the Transfiguration Monastery, locals generally sell a variety of home-prepared items, including *pirozhki* (small pies) stuffed with fish and whole smoked fish. The *pirozhki* are a favorite of the locals, who eat them year round. The smoked salmon is the best you will ever taste. The water up in this part of Ladoga is quite clean, so the salmon are delicious, especially after being smoked by local fisherman right after they catch them, which generally is the day before they sell them.

WHERE TO EAT ON VALAAM

At the ferry dock near the Transfiguration Cathedral are a few small wooden cafés. They don't look like much, but they offer a great chance to taste *kvas* brewed from locally baked black bread and *pirozhki* stuffed with locally grown vegetables or freshly caught fish.

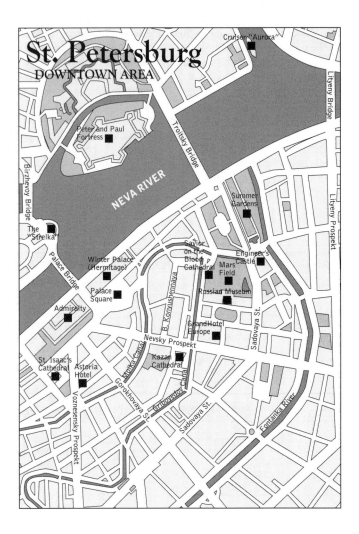

St. Petersburg
DOWNTOWN AREA

Cruiser "Aurora"

Lityeny Bridge

Troitsky Bridge

Peter and Paul Fortress

Birzhevoy Bridge

NEVA RIVER

Lityeny Prospekt

Summer Gardens

The "Strelka"

Palace Bridge

Winter Palace (Hermitage)

Savior on the Blood Cathedral

Engineer's Castle

Mars Field

Palace Square

B. Konyushennaya

Russian Museum

Admiralty

Sadovaya St.

GrandHotel Europe

Nevsky Prospekt

St. Isaac's Cathedral

Astoria Hotel

Kazan Cathedral

Voznesensky Prospekt

Gorokhovaya St.

Griboyedov Canal

Sadovaya St.

Fontanka River

Moika Canal

ST. PETERSBURG

ORIENTATION

Welcome to St. Petersburg turned Petrograd turned Leningrad turned St. Petersburg once again. Located on the Finnish Bay of the Baltic Sea, the second largest city in Russia is often considered by guests as one of the most magical cities they have ever visited.

HISTORY

In keeping with the megalomania inherent to Russia's most reputed rulers, Peter the Great hiked out to a marshy, mosquito-infested island in the delta of the Neva River on 16 May 1703, decided the location would be a perfect port for his future navy, cut two strips of soil from the earth, laid them in the shape of a cross and pronounced, "Here there shall be a city." In keeping with the ruthlessness inherent to Russia's most reputed rulers, he forced Swedish prisoners as well as destitutes from his own country to dredge the area, dig out a system of canals and lay foundations for initial structures. In keeping with the tyranny inherent to Russia's most reputed rulers, the tsar then compelled his subjects to come inhabit the place.

So goes the founding of St. Petersburg, a city "built on bones," a "window on the West," a thoroughly original European metropolis by virtue of its being preconceived and then executed according to that preconception. Peter wanted to be as close to Europe as possible, for after his eye-opening European tour of 1697, he decided he liked what was going on there more than what was happening in his homeland. But Peter could only be a tsar in Russia, so he decided to bring the West to him—and to his chagrined compatriots.

Despite ongoing war with nearby Sweden, Peter confidently forged ahead with development of his new city. In 1709 Russia defeated the Swedes at Poltava in the Ukraine, effectively winning the war and prompting Peter to proclaim, "Now the final stone has been laid in the foundation of St. Petersburg." Construction pressed on with a fury. Every inhabitant of the city was obliged to provide 100 stones per year to aid such projects as laying the main street, later called Nevsky Prospekt.

In 1710 the imperial family moved to St. Petersburg from Moscow, bringing with them most of the administrative institutions. In 1712 Peter declared St. Petersburg the new capital of Russia. To the Moscow aristocracy and merchant class the decree was horrifying—not so much because they lost the capital, but because they feared they would be induced to inhabit the uncivilized northern swamp of which their robust sovereign was so fond. And they were right. Given a choice between relocating or losing their heads, boyars and merchants reluctantly moved to the young city, where they were obliged to build large dwellings at their own expense. They were joined by 40,000 masons who had flocked to the city owing to Peter's decree forbidding building in stone anywhere but St. Petersburg. Life in the fledgling city was about as agreeable as most had expected. Floods routinely plagued the islands, and wolves roamed free after dark. Nevertheless, by the time of Peter's death in 1725 close to 100,000 people inhabited the city and 90 percent of Russia's foreign trade passed through it.

The first strides towards firmly establishing the city as a Western showcase were made by Empress Elizabeth (1741-61). Despite being as rambunctious as her father, Peter the Great, and being as indulgent as Imelda Marcos (Elizabeth owned 15,000 dresses), the empress founded the St. Petersburg Academy of Arts and commissioned Italian architect Rastrelli to build the Winter Palace and Smolny Cathedral.

A brief power struggle followed Elizabeth's death in 1761, with the German-born wife of Elizabeth's nephew Peter emerging to solidify her status as autocratix in 1762. Better known as Catherine the Great, she grabbed the Westernizing torch and ran with it. French became the official language of the court, Enlightenment ideas pervaded social circles and freedom of expression in arts and literature was encouraged (although in practice not fully tolerated).

By the 19th century St. Petersburg had succeeded in becoming the administrative and cultural center of the Russian empire. The city's population of nearly 600,000 was double that of the forgotten former capital, Moscow. Despite increasing despotism emanating from the Winter Palace, the golden age of Russian literature was born in St. Petersburg as novelists Dostoyevsky and Turgenev embarked on literary careers and poets Pushkin and Lermontov scribed their best verses before being killed in duels.

Although Tsar Alexander II emancipated the serfs in 1861, emerging radical groups such as the Populists and the Nihilists remained dissatisfied with the autocratic system and stirred up mass discontent. By the 1880s government officials, including the tsar, had become common targets for terrorist attacks. Alexander II didn't mind his back closely enough and was killed by a bomb in 1881 at the site of the present-day mosaic-covered Savior on the Blood Cathedral. By the end of the century factories had sprung up in the suburbs of St. Petersburg, drawing a large urban working class to the troubled capital. As the 20th century drew near, grumbling directed at the outdated and out-of-touch monarchy grew steadily louder.

On 9 January 1905 a peaceful congregation of 150,000 striking workers and families marched to Palace Square to hand Tsar Nicholas II a petition demanding basic civil rights and labor laws. Edgy troops opened fire on the crowd, killing thousands of unarmed citizens, including children. The confrontation became known as Bloody Sunday and put the writing on the wall for the doomed monarchy.

At the start of World War I in 1914 St. Petersburg shirked its German-sounding name and became Petrograd, a Russified version of the original. The war went badly for Russia from the outset, only intensifying unrest in the capital. That Nicholas had a domineering German wife who was influenced by a notoriously debauched religious charlatan named Rasputin didn't help the tsar's popularity. After mass strikes and demonstrations in anarchic Petrograd in February 1917, the tsar abdicated on 2 March 1917.

A provisional government set up shop in the Winter Palace but failed to satisfy anyone, including Bolsheviks led by Lenin and Trotsky. Bearing arms, the Bolsheviks took to the streets of Petrograd on 24 October 1917, storming the Winter Palace and establishing a new government. The political maneuvering that followed is a book in itself; suffice it to say that the Bolsheviks and Lenin proved not to be as dedicated to the peoples' will as they originally claimed. They in fact disbanded Russia's first democratically elected Constituent Assembly and seized absolute power by force when they did not win a majority of seats.

Petrograd lost its clout when Lenin moved the capital back to safer ground in Moscow after having given away the Baltic States as part of the 1918 Treaty of Brest. By 1920 two-thirds of Petrograd's population had vacated. Upon Lenin's death in 1924 the city was renamed Leningrad, which bothered no one, as lifelong residents had always called the city "Piter" anyway.

In the 1930s the more paranoid Josef Stalin became, the emptier became Leningrad. Ever suspicious of Petersburg's potential to stir up trouble, he ruthlessly purged the city of its military and political officials as well as other so-called threatening individuals. Stalin also included Leningrad in his push for Russia's mass industrialization, ordering more factories set up in its suburbs.

Rumors exist that the harrowing siege of Leningrad during World War II might have been "allowed" by Stalin, who saw the opportunity to save on TNT by letting the Germans desecrate the city for him. Whether or not the rumor is accurate, there is no disputing that the siege of Leningrad, known as "900 Days" (actually 872), was among the most horrific in history. From September 1941 to January 1944 the city was cut off from steady supplies of food, water, gas and electricity. Occasionally bread and ammunition were brought in by trucks that drove across the ice of Lake Ladoga's "Road of Life." Although the Ladoga route also enabled the evacuation of one million people, another one million Leningraders perished.

Although Leningrad received the best of the country's foodstuffs for a period after the war in gratitude for its grit, it was thanked by Stalin by being purged again from 1947-1953. Ever paranoid, especially about the solidarity that the war experience had created among Leningraders, Stalin put on show trials in which "traitors" confessed to fabricated crimes before being executed or sent off to perish in the GULAG. The steady depletion of the population did not exactly aid the Herculean task of rebuilding the city, which had lost one-third of its structures during the war.

The death of Stalin in 1953 finally gave Leningrad some breathing room to rebuild, repopulate and enjoy the "thaw" of the Khrushchev years. Not until the 1960s did the city's population reach pre-WWII levels.

During the humdrum Brezhnev era the city bided its time, slowly wasting away amidst Soviet self-deception like the rest of Russia. Moscow was clearly the center of the country, although innovations in music, art and literature continued to pour forth from more cultural Leningrad. The city welcomed Mikhail Gorbachev's *perestroika* and *glasnost*, electing a progressive mayor, Anatoly Sobchak, in 1990. The following year the city voted to change its name back to St. Petersburg, a gesture symbolic of the type of future the populace would like to embrace.

ABOUT THE CITY

St. Petersburg and Moscow have cultivated a historic rivalry. Muscovites consider Leningraders (as they still call St. Petersburg residents) rather snobbish, which is probably accurate, as citizens of St. Petersburg regard inhabitants of Moscow merely with pity.

Tsar Nicholas I once remarked that "St. Petersburg is Russian, but it is not Russia." Indeed the unique "Petersburg soul" is a frequently invoked distinction. If truth be told, however, the only noticeably distinguishing trait of modern-day St. Petersburg residents is a peculiar kind of arrogance that, as John Nicolson mentions in *The Other St. Petersburg* (1994), makes them consider "ambition as something you catch if you spend too much time in Moscow."

There certainly is something special about a city and a people that bask in soft northern light for twenty-four hours a day in summer and endure long, foreboding nights in winter. Occupying an area of 600 square kilometers, the city spreads itself on 42 separate islands interlaced with close to 70 canals and rivers spanned by some 300 bridges. Referred to as the "Venice of the North" (but resembling Venice only in the most generous of imaginations), the city lies on the same latitude as Alaska, yet its winter climate remains milder than Moscow's because of warming Atlantic air masses crossing the Baltic Sea.

The city itself is considered a museum of architecture, boasting over 200 stunning palaces and monuments, typically representing baroque or neoclassical styles. For cultural stimulation the population of almost five million chooses from over 50 museums, 20 theaters and concert halls, 60 stadiums and 4,500 libraries. For recreation inhabitants repair to dachas in the Karelian isthmus or to the countryside surrounding immaculate country palaces in the immediate environs. Industries include shipbuilding, heavy engineering, printing, brewing, textiles, electronics and tourism.

SIGHTS

Usually docking at St. Petersburg for two or three days, ships provide shore excursions that concentrate on the major city sights in addition to one of the country palaces. Brief synopses of the routinely visited attractions are here listed. Additional sightseeing ideas are suggested in The Inside Scoop.

Hermitage Museum

The Hermitage is the mother of all art museums. It boasts the biggest collection of artwork and antiquities in the world. In terms of sheer size and scope, it has only three rivals: the Louvre, the Prado and the Met. The holdings of the collection include some 12,000 sculptures, 15,000 paintings, 225,000 works of applied art, and over 600,000 drawings and prints. Spanning 400 of the Winter Palace's 1,057 rooms, the exhibition is made up of 2.8 million display pieces. It is said that to spend a few moments at each one would require nine years. And yet only a small percentage of the museum's entire collection is on view at any given time.

The Hermitage art collection was started by Peter the Great, who picked up a few Dutch maritime scenes while visiting Holland in 1697, first hanging them in his country palace at Peterhoff. Later, after acquiring more significant works, like a canvas by Rembrandt and a statue of Aphrodite, Peter began displaying the art in the Winter Palace (an earlier and much more modest version than the present one). Catherine the Great became the collection's greatest patron. Figuring that anyone who corresponds with Voltaire and Diderot ought to own some impressive art too, Catherine first bought a collection of 250 Dutch and Flemish paintings from a Berlin merchant who was short of cash. She purchased 600 more paintings from Count Brühl of Saxony in addition to procuring substantial portions of other European collections. Whenever her ambassadors traveled abroad, Catherine bade them to attend art auctions and buy, buy, buy!

Although no one person after Catherine went quite as bonkers over building the collection, Tsar Alexander I relieved Napoleon's wife Josephine of her entire art collection after France's defeat in 1814. Nicholas I, not to be outdone, bought the collection of Napoleon's stepdaughter. After the 1917 Revolution the Bolsheviks consolidated the museum's holdings by confiscating all of Russia's privately owned art collections. Only Stalin had the chutzpah to take from the collection, selling off a suite of Rembrandts and some Fabergé eggs for foreign currency.

The present-day museum complex, officially called the State Hermitage, comprises five structures: the Winter Palace, the Small Hermitage, the New Hermitage, the Old Hermitage and the Hermitage Theater. All buildings but the theater contain exhibits of the museum.

When the New Hermitage was completed in 1852 a limited public for the first time was allowed to view the collection. Prior to that, it had existed solely for imperial enjoyment, prompting Catherine to once write in a letter, "All this is admired by mice and myself." The Bolsheviks, after looting and vandalizing the Winter Palace in 1917, eventually cleaned up their mess, filled it with paintings and opened its doors to the public, calling it the Hermitage Museum.

Western European painting is presented with extreme breadth from the 13th century through the Renaissance up to post-impressionism. Impressionism is a major strength of the collection, owing to the efforts of two undaunted Russian aristocratic art patrons named Shchukin and Morozov. The two savvy art collectors befriended and supported Matisse and Picasso when the rest of Europe was too squeamish, also collecting work by Renoir, Monet, Pissarro and other present-day stars.

If surveying canvases by hero artists isn't your scene, the Winter Palace's gorgeous state rooms are sure to impress with their regal spaciousness, delightful color schemes and opulent adornment. Also, don't forget the rooms full of prehistoric, Egyptian, Oriental and classical antiquities, not to mention exciting temporary exhibitions. Yes, the place is huge, but you're in St. Petersburg, so you gotta go. Good luck.

St. Isaac's Cathedral

From the outside, St. Isaac's looks exactly like the fourth largest domed cathedral in the world that it is. Austerely regal by day and ominously imposing by night, the monstrous structure took forty years to build (1818–1858). The architect, a Frenchman named Montferrand, submitted 24 different plans in order to garner the commission. He labored his entire life on the project, redesigning as the structure's shortcomings or the tsar's new ideas periodically manifested. Just to prepare for the project an army of serfs laid 20,000 tree trunks to firm the site, and special ships and railways were built to haul granite pillars from Finland. By the time the 30,000-ton edifice was completed, building costs had exceeded by ten times those of the Winter Palace. Montferrand was so consumed by the project that he expired one month after he witnessed its completion. When his wife requested that he be buried within his beloved chef-d'œuvre, she was promptly rebuked and told to ship the body of her non-Orthodox hubby back to France.

Although the cathedral's gray marble exterior adorned with colonnades of red granite, gold-covered domes and bronze statues, is impressive, its interior is the main attraction. Fourteen varieties of marble, generous touches of jasper, malachite and gilded stucco, plentiful frescoes, mosaics and murals, in addition to a carved white marble iconostasis in front of a sanctuary illuminated by stained glass (an unusual feature in an Orthodox church) make for one of the most spectacular interior spaces you will see during your trip. A visit to St. Isaac's is not complete without hiking up to the colonnade surrounding the drum of the dome to behold an unrivaled panorama of the entire city. Acrophobes and claustrophobes not recommended.

Peter and Paul Fortress

In 1703 Peter the Great laid the first stone of the Peter and Paul Fortress, an outpost on tiny Hare's Island designed to defend against the Swedes. Although Peter defeated the Swedes without the aid of the fortress, its construction signaled the founding of St. Petersburg.

With the Swedes vanquished, what was Peter to do with such a brazen structure? Why, use it as a prison, of course. The first inmate was Peter's own son, Tsarevich Alexey, who was not at all like his father and was suspected of even plotting against the towering monarch. Peter set a precedent that was followed by practically all his successors, including Lenin, who sent the mutinous Kronstadt sailors here in 1921 before shipping them off to Siberia or the firing squad. Other famous naughty boys forced to spend time here were Catherine the Great's critic Alexander Radishchev, the whole lot of relatively tame Decembrist rebels and writers as diverse as Fyodor Dostoyevsky (whose death sentence was commuted as he awaited his turn in front of the firing squad), Maxim Gorky (who erred by peddling revolutionary leaflets under a tsarist regime) and Nikolay Chernyshevsky (who made the most of his incarceration by writing his fittingly titled treatise *What is to be Done?*).

In predictable juxtaposition, the Peter and Paul Cathedral, a shrine to the Romanov dynasty, stands nearby the bastions within which its opponents wasted impotently away. Built in a Dutch style more reminiscent of Protestant traditions than Orthodox ones (an idea of Peter, of course), the church's belfry supports the needlelike gilded spire that can be seen from all over the city. The church's interior, decorated in baroque and featuring a lovely carved iconostasis, houses the sarcophagi of the Romanov monarchs. Nicholas II, who was finally given a proper burial here in 1998, was interned in a nearby chapel because he was buried along with some of his non-royal servants. Peter the Great's tomb is easily discerned, as it is the only one topped by a bust of its occupant. Legend has it that Peter had his traitorous son Alexey buried beneath the aisle "so he would always be trampled on"; but don't believe every legend you hear.

Also of interest within the fortress are a functioning mint, a boathouse and a controversial statue of Peter the Great crafted by sculptor Michael Shemyakin in 1991. A cannon atop the Naryshkin Bastion (facing the Neva) traditionally is fired at noon, scaring the daylights out of tourists. On the other side of the bastion sunbathers in amusing, maximum-tan poses bake against the stone wall.

THE INSIDE SCOOP

As when in Moscow, the best bet for those wanting to tackle more than what is offered by shore excursions in St. Petersburg is to purchase a city-dedicated guidebook. For current cultural, entertainment and restaurant listings, consult the local English language newspaper *St. Petersburg Times* as well as the publications *Where* and *In Your Pocket*. These can be found most easily inside one of the big hotels such as Astoria, Grand Hotel Europe and Nevsky Palace.

Because of high docking fees, ships usually don't stay in St. Petersburg for much longer than two days. Such a brief visit to such an exciting city means two things: first, that organized shore excursions concentrate strictly on the main sights at a fairly brisk pace; second, that you might consider venturing off on your own to maximize your personal experience. As in Moscow, the ship is moored at some distance from the city center. You might want to avoid any needless bus rides back (such as for lunch), as the process cuts into a sizable portion of the day. The shore excursions themselves are discussed briefly below.

ALONG THE CANALS OF ST. PETERSBURG

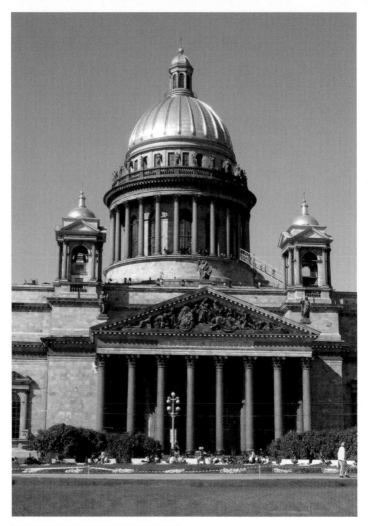

ST. ISAAC'S CATHEDRAL IN ST. PETERSBURG

THE "VENICE OF THE NORTH"

CATHERINE'S PALACE IN THE CITY OF PUSHKIN

Organized Shore Excursions

A **City Tour** is invariably conducted. It consists of a bus ride around the entire city with periodic stops at major sights for brief walks, picture-taking and souvenir-buying. Although it's a bummer being carted around on a bus, this tour is the best way to get a comprehensive overview of St. Petersburg. Some city tours include a stop at St. Isaac's Cathedral. It's likely that you won't have time to give the cathedral the time it deserves, so if such a stop amounts to your only visit, you might have to abandon the tour here or come back on your own. The tour generally also stops at the Peter and Paul Fortress and the dazzling Church of the Savior on the Blood.

The **Hermitage tour** provides the easiest access to and through the monstrous museum. Although it is entirely possible to visit the Hermitage on your own, the advantages of being with the tour group are that you skip the admission fee and long entrance lines, and you have your very own guide to impose a semblance of order on the madness that is the world's largest art collection.

Half-day trips to one of St. Petersburg's **country palaces** always are offered. Whether the destination is Pushkin (Tsarskoye Selo), Peterhoff (Petrodvorets) or Pavlovsk, the trip is worthwhile, as these former monarchs' estates are filled with as much history as any monument in the city center and surrounded by more beautiful landscaping than you'll see anywhere in Russia. The gardens and palace at Pushkin remind of Versailles; the gilded animated fountains of Peterhoff must be seen to be believed; and the homey opulence of Pavlovsk is a delight.

Evening excursions typically comprise outings to the ballet. A disappointing pill to swallow is that the world famous Mariinsky Theater (formerly the Kirov) is closed during summers while its dance troupe is off performing for foreign audiences. If your ship has arranged to visit the Hermitage Theater for ballet, consider yourself lucky, as this venue, a former private theater of the monarch, is exquisite and accessible only by special arrangement. Performances at other venues are usually put together for tour groups and are of varying quality, with folk shows running as a consistent favorite. The general problem with events such as ballets and symphonies is that most of the city's premier performing artists hit the road during the summer.

Other Possibilities

If you leave St. Petersburg without strolling its main lifeline, **Nevsky Prospekt,** you have failed to tap into the pulse of the city. Here is where the nouveau riche rub elbows with the nouveau homeless, where Soviet *stolovayas* (greasy spoons) neighbor chic restaurants and casinos, where visitors from around the world haggle with street artists and souvenir peddlers. During a two-hour jaunt along Nevsky you can eat a Russian ice cream, buy a coffee table art book, pick up a fashionable pair of shoes, mail a letter, exchange currency, get a haircut, have your portrait painted, scarf down a hot dog, buy some Alka-Seltzer and even make some new friends. Getting tired? Head to the café located in the Stroganoff Palace courtyard, at the corner of Nevsky and the Moika Canal.

Another absolute must is a **canal boat ride.** After all, would you go to Venice without taking a spin in a gondola? Okay, it's not quite the same thing, but a canal ride is the most enjoyable way to glimpse parts of the city you would never otherwise see from a vantage-point you would never otherwise get. If a canal ride is not one of your optional tours, you can hire a boat yourself where Nevsky Prospekt intersects either the Moika, Griboyedov or Fontanka Canals. For the pinnacle of romance, grab a friend and a bottle of champagne and take a midnight ride, which can be especially magical during the white nights of June and July.

For **further cultural explorations,** check out exhibitions at the Russian Museum at Ploshchad Iskusstv (just off Nevsky Prospekt) and the Marble Palace at 5/1 Millionaya ulitsa. For leisurely wanderings, try the famous Summer Garden, the setting of Peter the Great's marathon soirees, or the Alexander Nevsky Lavra, the burial site of tormented creative heroes such as Dostoyevsky, Tchaikovsky and Musorgsky. For something different, you could try the city's latest attraction, the Erotic Museum located in the Prostate Center at Furstatskaya 47/11, which has on display the penis of Rasputin, still bloated after all these years.

DINING IN ST. PETERSBURG

Aquarel (on the Petrograd side near the Birzhevoy Bridge, at Dobrolyubova Prospekt 14a). A floating restaurant with unbeatable views on the Winter Palace and the Neva embankment. The first floor café serves a wide range of Mediterranean dishes, including Italian standards and tapas, while upstairs serves Eastern and Continental cuisine in a slightly more formal setting.

Grand Hotel Europe (Michailovskiy street 1/7). You can do no wrong by visiting any of the restaurants connected to the best hotel in the city. The casual Sadko's is great for a burger; Chopsticks serves the best Chinese in the city; Rossi does first-rate Italian; the Caviar Bar is *de rigueur* for anyone requiring a fix of sturgeon; and l'Europe Restaurant is among the most regal places in the city to dine. Be it the burger or the sturgeon, it's going to cost you.

Hermitage Restaurant (Dvortsovaya Ploshchad 8). With an imperial location in the triumphal arch of the General Staff Building on Palace Square across from the Winter Palace and an interior comprised of a dozen separately themed dining rooms, this may just be the best place in the city to dine in style. Everything is done with spectacular attention to detail. Equally good for a romantic meal or a celebration with friends.

La Strada (Bolshaya Konyushenaya 27). If you feel like having pizza while in the center of town, there is no place better than this very relaxed split-level restaurant, only steps away from Nevsky Prospekt.

Staroye Café (Fontanka embankment 108). This cozy gem of a restaurant is a closely guarded secret by those in the know. We even debated telling you about it. Candlelit, full of antiques, with live but not intrusive jazz piano and cheap but delicious eats, you will remember your night spent here. It's very small, so you better call ahead: 316-51-11.

The Idiot (Moika 82). Bohemian, cozy and affordable, this Petersburg institution is a favorite of local artists, exchange students and all other fans of books (they have a small library here) and spirits (they serve you a complimentary shot of vodka). The Idiot is a standout in Petersburg for offering meatless versions of traditional Russian dishes, so it merits a pilgrimage by any self-respecting vegetarian.

Tinkoff (Kazanskaya 7). There is nothing particularly micro about this, the city's first microbrewery, featuring a sprawling main room with several adjoining drinking and dining areas, including a sushi bar. Think of it as the Gordon Biersch of Russia. Because the food, beer and atmosphere are excellent here, it can get crowded in the evenings, especially on the weekends.

ACCOMMODATIONS IN ST. PETERSBURG

As in Moscow, luxury accommodations can be prohibitive in St. Petersburg in the summer. And as in Moscow, the alternative to luxury is Soviet-era, which can be fun for those with spirit, but you're not going to get a recommendation here.

Angleterre (Bolshaya Morskaya 39). The little sister to the Astoria, located next door, is more affordable and a bit more retro, with some very nice rooms looking onto St. Isaac's Cathedral. They say the poet Yesenin hung himself in one of the rooms here, but Russians know better.

Astoria (Bolshaya Morskaya 39). Some feel that the regal Astoria, taken over by Rocco Forte in 1997, merits the title of the city's best hotel. We're not going to bicker, because everything in the historic hotel, where Hitler had planned to have his celebration dinner after conquering Leningrad (which he never did), from the famous main dining room to the guest rooms, is undeniably sumptuous and elegant.

Corinthia Nevskij Palace (Nevsky Prospekt 57). Somewhat businessman-oriented, this is still a top notch hotel, with a perfect location in a quiet atrium set back from Nevsky Prospekt. The Sunday brunch is the most decadent thing you will ever experience.

Grand Hotel Europe (Mikhailovskaya 1/7). Others will always try but will always fail to beat out this hotel as the city's undisputed best. With the most central location possible in the city, in a quiet lane off Nevsky Prospekt, a string of impeccable restaurants and thoroughly five-star service, they are forgiven for charging what they do.

Moika 22 (Moika embankment 22). Run by the Kempinski group, this latest addition to Petersburg's luxury hotel scene just may be the one that steals the Grand's thunder. The rooftop bar and restaurant, with an unparalleled panoramic view of the city may just be reason enough. But then there is the cozy café serving high tea, the wine bar, the free wireless Internet, the well-appointed rooms and the trademark Kempinski service.

Radisson SAS Royal (Nevsky Prospekt 49). Smack in the middle of Nevsky Prospekt, although miraculously with quiet rooms, this is wonderfully spiffy hotel that lives up to or even surpasses expectations of those familiar with Europe's Radisson SAS chain.

WATERWAYS

*Although the land distance between Moscow and St. Petersburg
is only 650 kilometers, the river route between the two cities
consists of 10 separate bodies of water. Among the waterways
traveled are Europe's largest lake, its longest river and the world's
longest man-made canal.*

*As you will learn, the Soviet government altered practically
every waterway along the route in order to facilitate easier travel
and gain sources of hydroelectricity. The Russian landscape is
still majestic, but at times it is difficult to refrain from informing
about the rather reckless manner in which it was modified.*

*So much forest was flooded, so many species of fish pushed
one step closer to extinction and so many human lives displaced
that it seems irresponsible not to provide a little history about
the formation of the present river network. As for the millions
of political prisoners (most of whom were accomplished authors,
professors and scientists ordered to toil to exhaustion by high
school drop-out commanders) who perished while being forced to
work on the undertakings, their plight merits remembrance.*

MOSCOW CANAL

A waterway from the Volga to Moscow is being made, which will make inland Moscow a port!
– *The Volga*, Soviet guidebook, 1932

Peter the Great dreamed of sailing unhindered from Moscow to St. Petersburg, a dream never fulfilled. Not until 1825 was the city of Moscow linked to the Volga—via a canal to the Moscow River. This first canal was built primarily to transport raw materials needed to build Moscow's Church of Christ the Savior, an architectural achievement later blown up by Stalin. Like the church, the canal had a limited lifetime, eventually suffering neglect at the hands of railroads.

Historically plagued by short water supply, Moscow by the 1930s needed to be linked to a major water source. Well water utilized in the 1700s had long dried up; spring water used in the 1800s had also been exhausted. A 1904 pipeline to the Moscow River provided relief for only about 25 years, after which the river was so depleted it could be crossed on foot in front of the Kremlin.

In the 1930s, with Stalin championing a relentless surge of technological advancement, no task was too grand for the industry of socialism. Russia's historical heart and soul, the Volga River, was targeted to solve Moscow's dilemma. Two routes for a canal from Moscow to the Volga were initially proposed. One followed existing streambeds and older canal alleys. Its advantage was ease of building; its disadvantage was its length (following the lay of the land, it tended to wind a bit). The other proposal more or less followed the bed of the Yakhroma River, joining the Volga west of the town of Dubna. Both proposals ultimately were rejected in favor of that of the present day canal, which bullies its way straight to the Volga in true Stalinist fashion.

Also true to Stalinist fashion, the endeavor was carried out with great haste and with absolute disregard for the lives of the GULAG prisoners who were forced to dig it out shovelful by shovelful. Like many enterprises undertaken during this period of Soviet technological expansion, the canal was built for subjects of the regime on the bones of subjects of the regime.

The feat, however, was undeniably awesome. The entire project required building 240 "complicated constructions," including seven concrete dams, eight earthen dams, 11 locks, eight hydroelectric plants, five pump stations, 15 bridges, two tunnels and the Northern River Passenger Terminal with its cargo port. During the five years of the canal's construction, workers excavated over 200 million cubic meters of earth and poured three million cubic meters of concrete along its 128 kilometers.

On 15 July 1937 inland Moscow woke up as a port connected by water to all of Russia's five major seas. The capital also gained a source of hydroelectricity as well as a new stretch of recreational areas.

Ship navigators appreciate the canal's reliable depth, straight course and wind-sheltered aspect. Passengers enjoy the canal's placidity, its occasional high banks and the vistas of countryside afforded by its elevated bed.

Engineering buffs might be interested to note some of the canal's special features, including round emergency towers protruding from the canal walls at various intervals. From these towers cables are able to raise an underwater concrete gate. These cut-off gates can dam up a section of canal for draining by a floating pump station and maintenance. Also of interest is that between Lock #2 and the reservoirs beyond Lock #6 the Volga waters are actually pumped through the canal.

The total time of passage from the Northern River Terminal to the Volga junction is approximately ten hours.

VOLGA RIVER

The Volga is Russia herself–her people, her history, her nature.
– Markov Yevgeniy, early century Russian writer

The Volga of the towpath is gone, replaced by a new, socialist Volga.
– People's Commissariat for Waterway Transit, 1932

It is time to stop the degradation of the Volga. Today is not too late. Tomorrow it is hardly possible.
– Social Committee to Save the Volga, 1989

From its remote source in the Valdai Hills northwest of Moscow the Volga River meanders up to the Rybinsk Reservoir, changes direction, commences winding southeast to Kazan before twisting westward to Volgograd, where it plunges finally southward to the Caspian Sea. Its 3,688-kilometer length makes it the longest river in Europe.

The rivership journey between Moscow and St. Petersburg explores only a fraction of the Volga's snaking course, bypassing much of what is referred to as the Volga region. Ships not traveling to Yaroslavl and Kostroma sail only 220 kilometers of the river–from the Moscow Canal to the Rybinsk Reservoir–while those making the side trip cover about 200 additional kilometers of upper Volga. Both these stretches comprise what chartmen call the "real Russian Volga," a region close to the river's source and endowed with as many quaint villages and neat plots of farmland as it is with colorful legends and tales.

The Volga is Russia's principal waterway, connected via a network of man-made canals to all five of the country's major seas. Half of all river freight in Russia is transported on its waters, which are also used to irrigate the steppes of the South. The river usually is navigable from March to mid-December. Early summer months can bring flooding, while in the later part of the summer low water levels expose shoals and sandbars.

The Greek philosopher Ptolemy first mentioned the Volga in the second century, comparing its grandeur to that of the Nile. By the eighth century Slavs were relying on the river as a trade route to the Middle East. During the flourishing of Kievan Rus in the 11th and 12th centuries, merchant settlements sprung up along the Volga's banks, and neighboring lands were cultivated. When Ivan the Terrible conquered Kazan and Astrakhan in the 16th century, the entire length of the river finally became the domain of a united Russia. Since that time the Russians have rightly believed that with the Volga intact the country is never conquered.

In the early 19th century the first Volga steamships appeared. In the 20th century the river was chopped into a chain of vast reservoirs in the socialist quest to supply the country with hydroelectricity. Most scientists today agree that the damming of the Volga turned out to be a colossal ecological as well as economic mistake. Not only was the filling of reservoirs carried out irresponsibly—forming large basins of flooded forests which destroy the ecosystem—but the flooding of valuable plowland ended up costing Russia much more than what it gained in electricity.

The Moscow–St. Petersburg journey misses the big Volga reservoirs (with the notable exception of the Rybinsk Reservoir). The stretches it does cover, perhaps somewhat more swollen than in the past, constitute parts of the river that still flow in their mischievous natural beds. A lone Volga fisherman in his rowboat in the soft twilight of dusk or sporadic campfires glowing amidst forested embankments in the dark of morning still reveal the majesty of the famed waterway that is said to flow in the heart of every Russian.

RYBINSK RESERVOIR

A man should have a sense of responsibility for all that people do and for the way they live.
– Lev Tolstoy

Before the formation of the Rybinsk Reservoir, great rivers such as the Volga, Sheksna and Mologa joined in a mire of ever-changing junctions, tributaries and rivulets on a vast plain settled by lively merchant communities. Here pumped the vital mercantile artery between the Russian north and south, connecting the rich northern forests with the fertile southern plains of the Volga and the Don.

There was a problem, though. The artery's blood ran thin in summer, the peak navigational period. Rivers, especially the Volga, dried so much they could be crossed without raising the leg of one's trousers. The locks of the Mariinskaya System were ill-equipped to solve the problem, as their capacity was limited by their size as well as by the shallow stretches between them. Often pulled from one lock to another with ropes, ships took up to three months to travel between Rybinsk and St. Petersburg.

Enter Josef Stalin and the "Big Volga" plan of 1932. Voting on an ambitious proposal to dam the Volga and Sheksna in order to create a massive reservoir, Stalin pronounced, "I am for it!" and sealed the fate of 700 villages that would be flooded. Documents reveal that, in true Stalinist fashion, "alternatives were not discussed." From the beginning the project was classified; the general public was not told of its blatant recklessness.

By 1936, when construction of the reservoir was in full swing, control of the project was turned over to Stalin's notorious Committee of Internal Affairs, which administrated the forced labor of GULAG prisoners. A laborer recalls the job site: "There were chains of guards everywhere. They watched all the prisoners, most of whom were charged with [political dissent]. They were very educated people. Maybe that's why they died the quickest—because it was more difficult for them to bear the unfairness of it. About 100 people died per day."

The filling of the reservoir began in 1941. As village families collected their belongings and began walking to unknown destinations, the flooding of over 4,000 hectares of fertile plowland commenced. After the water's initial brown murkiness settled, it eventually took on a greenish hue owing to floating vegetation. This substance, visible today, is actually the decay of submerged forests and depletes the water of its natural oxygen content. Rybinsk Reservoir, whose name derives from the word *ryba*, or "fish," becomes a larger and larger fish cemetery each year.

More than 60 rivers join the reservoir, which occupies an area of 4,500 square kilometers. Its vast size, not its average depth of only five meters, often earns it the name of Rybinsk Sea. The water can be turbulent at times, but buoys constantly broadcast weather conditions to ships' radios. Ships not diverting down the Volga to Yaroslavl and Kostroma cross the full length of the reservoir on a north-south axis. Those making the side trip likewise navigate the full length, but pass through the Rybinsk Hydroplant on the southeastern reach, thus entering and exiting the reservoir twice.

VOLGA–BALTIC CANAL

"We shall have whatever we need."
- Tsar Peter the Great

THE PAST: MARIINSKAYA CANAL SYSTEM

Between Lake Onega and the Rybinsk Reservoir ships navigate the Volga–Baltic Canal, opened in 1964. Before 1964 ships traveling between the two bodies of water navigated the locks and canals of the Mariinskaya System, a man-made waterway built by order of Peter the Great. The system was augmented and upgraded several times during the 19th century, yet its desired efficiency was always evasive. In the 1930s the Soviet government decided to completely overhaul the Mariinskaya System. Although several phases of the project were finished by 1940, most of the work was interrupted by World War II. Finally, in 1964, the Volga–Baltic Canal fully replaced the Mariinskaya System. Several segments of the old system, such as the canals around Lake Ladoga, Lake Onega and the White Lake, still operate but under minimal usage. Many of the 39 old wooden locks are still seen while sailing between St. Petersburg and the Volga.

THE PRESENT: VOLGA–BALTIC CANAL

The Volga–Baltic Canal is probably the most confusing part of the journey between Moscow and St. Petersburg because it is composed of several prominent and distinct bodies of water. They are (from south to north) the **Sheksna River,** the **White Lake,** the **Kovzha River,** the **Water Division Canal** and the **Vytegra Canal.**

The Soviets were fond of calling the 360-kilometer-long Volga–Baltic canal the longest in the world, even though its length does not entirely constitute man-made waterways. In fact the canal is comprised mostly of natural river and lake beds. However, by damming the constituent rivers and erecting hydroplants, the Soviets certainly altered existing waterways by carelessly flooding them, so in the final analysis perhaps the thing is man made after all. It is made up of eight locks and hydroelectric stations as well as numerous dams, reservoirs and bridges. A significant if not somewhat unintelligible feature of the canal is that it connects the slopes of the Baltic Sea and Caspian Sea water basins. Upon completion, the canal, naturally, was named after Lenin.

The landscape of the Volga–Baltic Canal region is alternately enchanting and graceless. At times the canal narrows to such an extent that foliage on the banks practically brushes the hull of the ship; at other times the banks disappear altogether into murky expanses of flooded forest. Some stretches present quaint villages of carved cottages adjacent to fields of rye, oat, barley or flax; in other places industrialized towns confront the river with gray jungles of mills and machinery. Dense deciduous and coniferous forests endow the region with a dark majesty but also provide it with economic sustenance by disappearing at the spinning teeth of roaring chain saws. Timber yards, wood freighters, storehouses and mills are noticeable all along the canal. At last check, forests still occupied two-thirds of the region.

Wildlife that might be spotted amidst the trees include such sizable creatures as moose and elk. In the water swim pike, perch, bream and burbot.

Sheksna River (186 kilometers)

Connecting the Rybinsk Reservoir to the White Lake, the Sheksna River is composed of three segments: the Upper Sheksna (52 kilometers), the Sheksna Reservoir (66 kilometers) and the Lower Sheksna (68 kilometers). The former two segments are separated from the latter by a dam at the Sheksna Hydroplant and are often together referred to as the Sheksna Reservoir. The name Sheksna is thought to be derived from a Finnish term meaning "a sedge-covered tributary." Ever since the times of Kievan Rus, when brave men-at-arms battled its rapids, this sedge-lined tributary has played a vital role by connecting the northern lands to the Volga.

The original construction of the Mariinskaya System left the Sheksna completely intact. Subsequent upgrading called for straightening the riverbed and incorporating a network of locks. The Volga–Baltic Canal called for more alterations, such as substantial widening and deepening of parts and the implementation of a hydroplant. Vast areas of forest were flooded and now make up much of the riverside landscape, especially along the reservoir proper.

White Lake

Mention of the ancient White Lake is frequent in Russian history and folklore. Ever since its shores were settled by Veps tribes in the eighth century, the lake has served as a trade bridge between Russia's north and south. In the 17th century the lake was known as the "tsar's fishing grounds" because government boats cruised around enforcing a fish tax on all fishermen save those from nearby monasteries. (Tsars knew that taxing God's representatives was bad karma.)

The lake was incorporated into the Mariinskaya System in the 19th century and subsequently into the Volga–Baltic Canal. Like the canal's natural rivers, the lake did not escape manipulation. It was used to absorb the overflow of the Sheksna River, a role that influenced its natural currents and flooded portions of its shores. The circular shoreline, formed over a period of thousands of years, suddenly disappeared, and decaying, submerged forests soon endangered the underwater ecosystem. An ecological station was recently set up in the lakeside city of Belozersk to monitor the lake and heal the wounds inflicted on it by the Volga–Baltic Canal's construction.

A host of rivers flows into the White Lake, contributing to its 1,400 square kilometer area. Only one river, the Sheksna, drains the lake. The lake bottom is uniformly flat and sandy, making for a consistent depth of five meters. Northern winds occasionally induce sizeable daytime swells, while fogs can creep in and cover the lake during still nights.

Kovzha River (43 kilometers)

Between the Water Division Canal and the White Lake the Kovzha River runs more or less in its historical bed. In formerly winding places the river's course has been redirected, but spots like the Konstantinovskiye

Rapids, at the northern end of the river, still retain their shallow and rocky formidableness. Because so many other rivers and streams feed into the Kovzha, damming caused its banks to overrun extensively. Nevertheless, its wide areas of flooded forest as well as its occasional tree-lined narrow necks lend the Kovzha landscape a sense of remote if not wistful splendor.

Water Division Canal (53 kilometers)

Certainly better than what Peter the Great had in mind, this narrow canal, dug in 1963, at last joined the Vytegra and Kovzha Rivers without the use of locks. Peter, of course, did not have access to the dredges and excavators the Soviets used to push around over 31 million cubic meters of earth. The reason for the canal's name is that it officially marks the joining of Russia's sheer northern slope with its sloping southern one, forming a plateau of sorts between the Baltic and Caspian water basins.

Vytegra Canal (38 kilometers)

This segment consists of a 13-kilometer-long canal and three subsequent reservoirs. The canal portion, being narrow and shallow, requires navigators' close attention. Because of its frequent usage and clay bottom, its water often is dark brown. The Vytegra region is known for its timber output, which includes an unusually resonant variety of fir used for crafting musical instruments. It was here on a forested hillside (now an island in one of the reservoirs) that Peter the Great spent ten days consulting with engineers and scratching his head over the dilemma of connecting the Vytegra and Kovzha Rivers.

LAKE ONEGA

Resembling a one-clawed lobster, Lake Onega spans a 10,000-square- kilo-meter area, making it the second largest lake in Europe, bowing in size only to its twice-larger neighbor, Lake Ladoga. Depths of the lake average 30 meters, but include cavities reaching as far down as 120 meters. More than 50 rivers and 1,000 streams feed Onega, but only the Svir River, which connects it to Ladoga, originates from Onega. The lake contains over 1,300 islands, most of which lie in the north, where forests of pine stand at the edges of rocky, jagged coastline. Linden and elm trees are more common along the southern areas, where sandy shores slope into shallow bays of reeds.

Primitive tribes from as early as the first century are among those who have inhabited the shores of Lake Onega. (Petroglyphs found on the cliffs of its eastern shores are on view in St. Petersburg's Hermitage Museum.) The lake sustains more than 40 species of fish, including formidable freshwater salmon and trout. Bays are home to some 200 varieties of birds, including ducks, swans, cranes and geese. Prowling through the surrounding forests are bears, elks, foxes, wolves, hares and squirrels. Doing more paddling than prowling, muskrats are also prominent; how they got here from North America no one knows.

The purity of the dark Lake Onega water is practically unsurpassed, second only to distilled water.

The lake's location in the rugged northern republic of Karelia makes for a severe climate. Air temperatures dip below freezing for half of the year, and frequent storms can generate swells as high as five meters, although your rivership is not allowed to enter the lake when the waves are higher than 2.5 meters.

Onega's misty dawns of June and autumnal symphonies of shoreline colors never cease amazing thousands of annual visitors, many of whom come to behold the miraculous wooden churches on Kizhi Island.

SVIR RIVER

The Svir River stretches 215 kilometers through northern forests below Karelia, connecting Europe's two largest lakes, Ladoga and Onega. The Svir landscape, rugged and majestic, cannot help but entrance the shipboard observer. At times the banks take on the form of reddish, forested precipices; at others, they slope smoothly into verdant marshes.

Ever since the first settlements appeared along the Svir over 5,000 years ago, the region has been considered severe and wild. Even during the 13th century, when Mongol-Tatar domination caused exoduses from cities, few settlers dared to venture into the area's impenetrable forests and foggy marshlands. During tsarist times the Svir region was a place of exile; during the communist era it was targeted for hydropower.

The Svir and its forests have always provided Russia with timber. Even today the main occupation of those living along the Svir is lumbering. Log piles, timber rafts and storage sheds can be seen all along the river and its thirty tributaries. Pine and fir trees still line the shores, for they preserve the banks and regulate water level.

The river's depth reaches five meters in autumn and ten meters in spring. (The water level is actually regulated by the demands of the river's two hydroplants.) The river usually freezes from December to April, but during mild winters it may not totally solidify. From the water local fishermen reel in salmon, trout and pan fish. The brownness of the water is due to the flooding of the banks caused by the Svir's two hydroplants.

Somewhat of a nightmare from a navigational standpoint, the Svir is plagued by shallow stretches, narrow rapids, blind bends, dense fogs and the constant threat of floating debris such as tree trunks and coagulations of peat. During the first half of this century riverboat captains relied on wooden navigational buoys, which were not entirely reliable, as the kerosene lamps within had to be lit by hand from a rowboat. Today all 1,070 modern buoys are lit automatically.

LAKE LADOGA

Covering 18,000 square kilometers and containing 900 cubic kilometers of water, Lake Ladoga resembles a sea more than a landlocked body of freshwater. Known for a moody temperament and surrounded by austere beauty, Europe's largest lake can challenge the nautical sense of a river captain as well as the visual sense of a first-time visitor.

Ladoga is characterized by extremes. Depths in the north reach 230 meters, while in the south, shallow and rocky areas can impede navigation. The landscape of its rugged northern shores comprises sheer, jagged precipices and sharply cut bays; these features likewise define the north's 500 remote islands and skerries. By contrast, southern shores constitute sloping, sandy beaches on both sides of the lake's 130 kilometer width. More than 30 rivers supply Ladoga with water; yet only one river, the Neva, flows from it.

Baltic salmon and sturgeon are among the numerous species of fish inhabiting Lake Ladoga. One of the more anomalous species of wildlife is the Ladoga seal, an ancient creature which migrated from the White Sea.

Historically, Ladoga has supported not only a diverse northern ecosystem but also the inhabitants of its closest metropolis, St. Petersburg. During the WWII siege of Leningrad, food rations and supplies were transported and residents evacuated on the frozen lake's "Road of Life."

Today Lake Ladoga continues to sustain St. Petersburg—by supplying the city with drinking water. Unfortunately, the lake is close to biological death thanks to phosphate pollution caused by the lakeside industrial town of Priozersk. Moreover, in 1990 divers discovered a shipwreck that had lain on the lake bed for thirty years leaking radioactivity.

The only threat Lake Ladoga poses to the visiting rivership passenger is rough water in late summer, although as with Onega, riverships are forbidden to enter when the waves are over 2.5 meters.

NEVA RIVER

Starting from Lake Ladoga, the Neva runs a total of 74 kilometers to the Finnish Bay of the Baltic Sea, where it fans out into a 280-square-kilometer basin. The name of the river is derived from the Finnish word *nevo*, for "marshy," which is an adequate description of its massive estuary. First claimed for Russia by the Novgorod principality in the ninth century, the Neva was always a bone of contention between the Swedes and Russians. Peter the Great finally consolidated Russia's claim to the river with his victory over Sweden in the Northern War of 1700-21. To show his intention of holding onto the river, he founded his new capital, St. Petersburg, at its mouth.

The Neva remains an integral part of St. Petersburg, which spreads atop 42 of the river's islands and is divided by a system of river-fed canals. Although this orientation creates an effect reminiscent of Venice or Amsterdam, historically it has meant lots of flooding. While walking around St. Petersburg you might occasionally spy a plaque showing the water level in the city during some of the more devastating floods, such as those of 1824 and 1924.

The voyage by rivership between St. Petersburg and Lake Ladoga is quite scenic, as the Neva flows through dramatically high banks and varies in width from 250 to 1,300 meters. Depths along the way range from eight to 24 meters. The current moves at an average speed of four kilometers per hour, except at a bottlenecked section called the Ivanovskiye Rapids, where the pace quickens. Because of the river's proximity to the Baltic Sea, its surrounding climate tends to be damp and rainy. Even during the peak summer month of July the temperature on the water rarely reaches above 25° centigrade (78° Fahrenheit).

TOPICS OF INTEREST

To enhance your enjoyment and understanding of the sights you will be touring and the information you will be assimilating, read here about major topics like Russian history, architecture and religion. You will also find advice to help you become a knowledgeable souvenir shopper.

A word about the Russian calendar: In 1700 Peter the Great finally replaced Russia's old Byzantine calendar with the Julian calendar, a more effective version used in Western Europe since 1582. Peter's timing was bad, though, for shortly after his decree, Europe changed to the even more effective Gregorian calendar (the one in use today). Russia didn't follow suit, as usual, and by the 20th century it found itself lagging a full two weeks behind the rest of the world. The Soviets finally straightened the matter out by adopting the Gregorian calendar in 1918. That year, January 31 was decreed to be February 14. This discrepancy explains why the Soviets celebrated the October Revolution in November. Because Orthodox holidays are still based on the Julian calendar, Russians to this day celebrate Christmas on January 7.

In this book events are dated according to the calendar officially in use in Russia at the time. In other words, the Julian calendar is used before 1918 and the Gregorian thereafter. This method of documenting Russian history is the most common, so don't feel you've been cheated out of two weeks like those poor folks in 1918.

RUSSIAN ARCHITECTURE

While visiting Moscow, St. Petersburg and the provinces, you encounter architectural styles ranging from Byzantine to medieval to Old Russian to baroque to neoclassical to art nouveau. That's great, but what does it all mean?

CHURCH ARCHITECTURE

Because the Russian Orthodox Church descends from Constantinople, church architecture in Russia has its roots in Byzantine traditions. The Chronicles state that Russian ambassadors to Constantinople were so taken by that city's churches that they reported, "We did not know if we were in heaven or on earth...we only knew that there, God is present among men." Accordingly, the first church structures in Kiev (the first center of the Russian Church) emulated Constantinople's.

Although Russian churches evolved on their own, their initial layout remained faithful to that of mid-Byzantine churches. The design is called **cross-in-square,** which in simplest terms means that the building is essentially square, divided by the shape of a broad cross into nine bays, or sections, including the large center bay which forms the church's nave, or main interior space. The central bay is crowned by a large dome. Smaller domes often are situated over the four corner bays. Inside, pews and statues are absent, while frescoes and icons abound. The exit is always to the west and always beneath a rendering of the Last Judgment—a guilt trip to go, if you will.

As cultural, religious and political activities moved from Kiev to the northern regions of Novgorod, Vladimir and Pskov in the 12th and 13th centuries, the domes became more pointed, most likely to facilitate snow runoff. These helmet domes became separated from the roof itself by windowed cylinders called drums. In order to keep out the cold, the windows on the drums grew steadily narrower as the **drums** themselves grew longer. By and by the cupolas stretched increasingly heavenward, and the bulbous **onion dome** was born.

This period also saw the genesis of another distinctly Russian architectural element, the **kokoshnik** gable. Curved gable-ends were incorporated below the roof's central drum, which created the effect of a stepped pyramid starting at the roofline and terminating at the top of the cupola. These arch-like gable-ends gradually became slightly pointed, perhaps to mimic the shape of the cupola itself, but not to imitate the Gothic arch, as is often assumed. This element reached maturity once the political tide shifted to Moscow, where the decorative arches were arranged in ascending tiers, forming the uniquely Russian *kokoshniky* which lead the eye upward to the cupola. The Annunciation Cathedral in the Moscow Kremlin is one of many churches you will see that make splendid use of *kokoshnik* gables.

The cross-in-square layouts eventually were augmented with adjoining chapels, exterior galleries, porches and often a tent-shaped belfry. These additions, in combination with the elements mentioned above, came to form what is commonly referred to as traditional Russian church architecture. Attention-grabbing St. Basil's Cathedral on Red Square, often considered the embodiment of traditional Russian style, was at the time of its construction actually an unparalleled departure from convention. Essentially a tent-shaped church (i.e., spire-like rather than utilizing drums and domes) amidst a conglomeration of distinct chapels, St. Basil's represented an eclectic and unprecedented mix of elements seen earlier only on wooden churches.

SECULAR ARCHITECTURE

Peter the Great altered the course of Russian architecture by forbidding building in stone anywhere but his new city of St. Petersburg, where only Western-style structures were allowed. This shift away from concentrating on church architecture in favor of secular structures spelled the beginning of baroque in Russia.

The initial **Petrine baroque** was rather restrained in that it remained based on north-European prototypes rather than on Western baroque structures, with their exuberant decoration, curvaceous forms and complex spatial arrangements. Good examples of Petrine baroque in St. Petersburg are Peter's yellow Summer Palace in the Summer Garden as well as Menshikov's Palace and the red-brick St. Petersburg University building, both on the Neva embankment.

Under Empress Elizabeth (1741-61), Russian baroque reached its peak. Directed by Russian as well as European architects—most notably Italian Bartolomeo Rastrelli—the city's building projects, including the grandiose Winter Palace and the palace at Peterhoff, became more truly baroque. St. Petersburg's Smolny Cathedral, started by Rastrelli, is an intriguing example of this period in that it incorporates traditional Russian onion domes into a dominant baroque design. Had Rastrelli finished the cathedral, examples of **rococo** motifs would have been added. As it turned out, Elizabeth eventually ran out of funds, so true rococo features never really made it into Russia.

Elizabeth's bankruptcy brought the baroque period in Russia to an abrupt halt. Catherine the Great (1762-96) championed Russia's next sweeping architectural phase, **neoclassicism.** The empress commissioned large-scale buildings that were a reaction to the frippery of late baroque and favored a more simple approach to building, as attained by the early Greeks. The dominant belief was that society as well as architecture are at their best in their purest forms. Thus a return to the classical orders and to strict geometric shapes was exhibited in new buildings throughout the country.

Although true classical purity of either society or architecture was never really regained, neoclassical architecture dominated Russian cities such as Kostroma, Yaroslavl and most prominently, St. Petersburg. The latter became one of the most consistently neoclassical cities in Europe. Today its colored stucco facades with details picked out in white still create a sense of grandiose theatricality.

Russia's attention turned back to Moscow after the 1917 Revolution. Although interesting **art nouveau** work was demonstrated there on such buildings as the Metropol Hotel, the city soon was ruthlessly remodeled to reflect the triumphant march of socialism spearheaded by Stalin.

So-called **social realist** buildings relied on heavy classical motifs. Streets were bulldozed and widened to create huge boulevards and squares fit for grand proletarian pageants.

Among the most bizarre architectural styles to be seen in Russia is that dubbed **Stalinist Gothic,** exhibited chiefly by seven ominous skyscrapers planted about Moscow. The Northern River Terminal, with its towering, red star-capped spire is also representative of this Gotham City look, which Stalin borrowed from early New York skyscrapers.

Unimaginative reconstruction plagued many Russian cities besides Moscow after the damage inflicted on them by World War II. With ecclesiastical architecture abolished and civic structures executed in an uninspired fashion dictated primarily by modern construction methods, the last notable albeit dubious contribution to Russian architecture was the mercilessly drab, prefabricated blocks of concrete that provided cramped residential space to Soviet citizens. Dubbed *khrushchevky* after Nikita Khrushchev, the Party leader whose term in office saw their completion, these ill-constructed and often unfinished apartment complexes had the effect of blighting city landscapes and making Soviet citizens pine for the integrity of earlier neoclassical structures or even the spaciousness of Stalin-period architecture.

ORTHODOX RELIGION

The best way to avoid the doldrums sometimes caused by visiting so many Or-
thodox churches and monasteries is to arm yourself with a little knowledge about
the religion itself. Here is a brief overview of the Church's evolution.

Notwithstanding a 70-year hiatus during Soviet times, the practices of
Eastern Orthodoxy have defined Russian spirituality and pervaded Russian social, cultural and political life since the 10th century. The Russian
Orthodox Church is the largest single branch of the Eastern Orthodox
religion, which numbers over 125 million followers and spans primarily
across Eastern Europe and parts of the Middle East.

Before the 10th century Slavs and other tribes inhabiting present-
day Russia and Ukraine carried out pagan traditions, oriented around
respect for and harmony with the forces of nature. The unifying belief was
that everything in the universe is interconnected and that humankind
must unobtrusively take its place among a natural order that functions
according to powers much greater than human will.

It was the idea of Grand Prince Vladimir I (980-1015) to introduce
monotheism to Kievan Rus as part of his efforts to unify a growing
domain divided by clans and self-contained communities. According
to legend, Vladimir, not knowing which monotheism was best, tried
on the tenets of various religions to see how they suited his personal
taste and political aims. He pondered Judaism but thought it too geo-
graphically scattered; he summarily dismissed the Muslim faith (even
though it allowed harems) because it forbade alcohol; and he found
Roman Christianity unappealing because the Pope claimed political
precedence over secular princes such as himself. In the end the matter
was settled when Vladimir married the sister of the Byzantine emperor,
thus becoming aligned with Eastern Christianity, which had developed
in Constantinople independently from Rome ever since 330 AD.

Vladimir persuaded the patriarch of Constantinople to send envoys to Kiev in 988, and the Russian Orthodox Church was founded. The religion brought with it Byzantine influences in culture, art and architecture which were to contribute to the formation of the Russian identity for the next 1,000 years.

In 1300 the seat of the Russian Church moved from Kiev to Vladimir. Twenty years later it moved to Moscow, where it still is located today. Although no central governing body presides over the Church, the holy patriarch of Russia (Alexiy II at present) is its highest official. A council called the Holy Synod helps in the administration department. The patriarch lives at the Church's headquarters in the St. Daniil Monastery in Moscow, although Church business is now increasingly conducted at the Trinity Monastery of St. Sergius (formerly Zagorsk), just outside Moscow.

Perhaps never before in history has Christianity been so boldly and summarily suppressed as during Soviet rule in Russia. Accusing the Church of being as ideologically oppressive as the monarchy as well as fundamentally antithetical to communist ideology (not to mention being a capitalist enterprise), the Bolsheviks in 1917 closed all churches and instituted prohibition on religion. Over the next several decades more than 90,000 churches were either blown up or ruinously neglected. Of those 7,000 or so that remained standing, many were put to secular use, housing workshops, storage or swimming pools. Particularly significant monasteries and churches were converted into "museums of national cultural history."

In 1988 the Orthodox Church celebrated its millennium by retaining its legal status in Russia. Since then, the government has been steadily returning to the Church all structures confiscated by the Soviets. Religious services have commenced once again throughout the country and are attended by armies of impoverished *babushkas* as well as enterprising politicians. Over 50 million Russian, Byelorussian and Ukrainian citizens have officially rejoined the Church. Parents once again baptize their babies and take their children to Sunday schools.

RUSSIAN LEADERS

While touring Russia you are sure to hear the names of its mighty leaders thrown around in connection with events, foundings and historical periods. Indeed everything composing Russian history seems to be inextricably connected to its rulers, as autocracy and dictatorship have determined the direction of the country throughout its existence. To help clarify the historical information you'll receive along the way, a comprehensive chronology of rulers is here provided.

Rurik of Novgorod (862-79) Norseman who founded Novgorod, thus giving birth to the Russian state and the Rurik dynasty.

Oleg of Kiev (879-912) Moved the capital from Novgorod to Kiev, setting the stage for city rivalry that divided the country until 1478.

Igor (912-46) Exacted heavy taxes on Slavs, who tied him to two trees and ripped him in half.

Olga (946-69) Widow of Igor. First ruler to be baptized by Orthodox Church, then in Constantinople.

Svyatoslav (969-72) A great warrior who conquered Bulgaria but neglected domestic affairs and ultimately was murdered.

Yaropolk (972-80) Killed his brother in a power struggle and later was murdered by half-brother Vladimir.

Vladimir I (980-1015) Established Russian Orthodox Church and strengthened Russia. Maintained a harem of five wives and countless concubines and was later canonized.

Yaroslav the Wise (1015-54) Well-educated warrior and diplomat who fostered a cultural golden age in the capital of Kiev.

Various rulers (1054-1113) Sons of Yaroslav and other would-be heirs fought amongst themselves, with power being passed around.

Vladimir II Monomakh (1113-25) Benevolent ruler who took power at age sixty and united northern and southern principalities.

Various rulers (1125-55) Squabbling amongst brothers and cousins divided the country once again and resulted in six short reigns.

Yury Dolgoruky (1155-57) A power-hungry sort who founded Moscow and was later poisoned to death by his enemies.

Various rulers (1157-69) Power struggles resulted in three or four short reigns and the burning of Kiev.

Andrey Bogolubov (1169-74) Moved the capital from Kiev to Vladimir. Behaved unkindly to boyars, who later killed him and sacked his city.

Vsevolod III (1176-1212) Known as the Big Nest because of his large family. Strengthened the Vladimir–Suzdal principality, still the seat of the divided empire.

Various rulers (1212-52) Descendants of Vsevolod were neutralized as invading Mongols massacred the Russian people and sacked their cities, establishing Golden Horde domination.

Alexander Nevsky (1252-63) Famous warrior who defeated the Swedes on the Neva before being installed as grand prince. Was poisoned to death by Mongol-Tatars and later canonized.

Various rulers (1263-1328) Relatives of Alexander Nevsky alternately took power and/or were killed as the Golden Horde manipulated family feuds.

Ivan I (1328-41) Known as "the Moneybags." Was installed as grand prince in the new capital of Moscow. Placated the Golden Horde by being a good tax collector while embezzling on the sly.

Semyon (1341-53) Intended to abate future power struggles by decreeing that only sons of princes were legitimate heirs. Unfortunately, he had no sons when he died of plague.

Ivan II (1353-59) Brother of Semyon. Managed to leave behind a son.

Dmitry Donskoy (1359-89) Heroic ruler who handed the Golden Horde their first defeat, at Kulikovo. Wasn't canonized until 1989.

Vasily I (1389-1425) Continued to resist Mongol-Tatars. Instituted last names for Russians, although his is unknown.

Vasily II (1425-62) Known as "the Dark" because he was blinded by an opponent for paying an excessive sum to the Golden Horde to release him after being captured in battle.

Ivan III [the Great] (1462-1505) Stood up to the crumbling Golden Horde, ending Russia's subjugation. Unified the Russian lands at last and built the Moscow Kremlin.

Vasily III (1505-33) Mopped up remaining independent principalities for Muscovy. Has the dubious distinction of being Ivan the Terrible's father.

Ivan IV [the Terrible] (1533-84) First ruler to take the title of tsar. Paranoid and murderous, he saved historical face by conquering Kazan, Astrakhan and much of Siberia.

Fyodor I (1584-98) Feeble-minded son of Ivan IV. Was a mere figurehead while brother-in-law Boris Godunov ruled the country. His death ended the Rurik dynasty.

Boris Godunov (1598-1605) Allegedly orchestrated the murder of Fyodor's brother, Tsarevich Dmitry, gaining the throne and setting the stage for the Time of Troubles.

False Dmitry I (1605-06) Claimed he was Tsarevich Dmitry, alive after all. Mustered an army and stormed Moscow, taking the throne. Was eventually killed and, in a symbolic gesture, shot out of a cannon.

Vasily Shuisky (1606-10) Boyar who organized an army and ousted False Dmitry I. Upset by the appearance of a second pretender, he had the real Dmitry exhumed and brought to Moscow.

False Dmitry II (1608-10) Also claiming to be Tsarevich Dmitry, he commenced to rule from a camp outside of Moscow but was soon killed by loyalists.

Throne vacant (1610-13) The Time of Troubles reached its peak when the Poles occupied Moscow. They were eventually ousted by a Volga region army led by Minin and Pozharsky.

Michael Romanov (1613-45) A young boyar distantly related to Ivan IV, he accepted the throne at the behest of a popular assembly. The first ruler of the Romanov dynasty.

Alexey (1645-76) Known as "the Quiet." Annexed the Ukraine and put down Stepan Razin's famous peasant revolt, apparently without making much noise.

Fyodor III (1676-82) Has the distinction of being the half-brother of Peter the Great.

Ivan V (1682-96) As a sickly boy he shared the throne with Peter I, although the country was ruled by the boys' sister Sofia until Peter matured and elbowed her out.

Peter I [the Great] (1682-1725) Turned Russia into a prominent European power and delivered her from cultural backwardness. Founded St. Petersburg, established the navy, won the Northern War, shaved beards, was fond of beheading, died of a bladder infection.

Catherine I (1725-27) Peter's wife. She left the ruling up to Peter's right-hand man, Menshikov.

Peter II (1727-30) Peter's grandson. Never ruled from the capital, staying in Moscow after his coronation. Died of smallpox shortly thereafter.

Anna (1730-40) Peter the Great's niece. Surrounded herself with foreign advisors and executed opponents by the thousands. Decadent and repressive, she ran up the national debt by throwing lots of parties.

Ivan VI (1740-41) Unfortunate two-month-old tsar who was ousted in a coup and exiled. He was imprisoned later at Shlisselburg and killed during a failed rescue attempt.

Elizabeth (1741-61) Peter the Great's daughter. Half-heartedly carried on her father's reforms. Was adored by the court for her excesses—she owned 15,000 dresses and liked to party all night.

Peter III (1761-62) Relieved the nobility of compulsory 25-year state service, creating a privileged leisure class. Was ousted in a coup by his shrewd wife, the future Catherine II.

Catherine II [the Great] (1762-96) Increased Russia's cultural sophistication and power. Continued Westernization. Flirted with lifting repressions. Flirted with everything (though the horse rumor is doubtful).

Paul (1796-1801) Catherine's son. Despised his mother and attempted to reverse her liberal policies. Was strangled in a palace coup sanctioned by his son, the future Alexander I.

Alexander I (1801-25) Was preoccupied with foreign affairs, including Napoleon's invasion. He beat the French in 1812 by leaving them in Moscow right before winter.

Nicholas I (1825-55) Put down the Decembrists' revolt and thereafter ruled with an iron fist. A despot *par excellence*, he even declared himself Pushkin's personal censor.

Alexander II (1855-81) Freed the serfs and pushed through a few other reforms. Failed to satisfy emerging radical groups, though, and was killed by a bomb.

Alexander III (1881-94) A reactionary ruler, likely influenced by his father's assassination. Passed anti-Semitic laws and watched Russia's industrialization foster worker malcontent.

Nicholas II (1894-1917) The last tsar. Blundered on Bloody Sunday, the Russo–Japanese War, WWI, as well as internal affairs. Was shot in Siberia along with his entire family soon after abdicating.

V. I. Lenin (1917-24) Engineered the 1917 Revolution and founded the world's first socialist state. He championed true communism yet quickly resorted to dictatorship. Privately referred to Russians as "fools."

Josef Stalin (1929-53) Brought the USSR to the forefront of industrialized nations, survived WWII and committed mass genocide that made Hitler's seem unambitious.

Nikita Khrushchev (1957-64) Denounced Stalin and embarked on limited human rights reforms. Blundered in foreign affairs, couldn't help the economy and was "retired."

Leonid Brezhnev (1964–82) Un-denounced Stalin and put an end to reforms. Thrived on bureaucracy and spirits as Soviet society steadily collected dust.

Yury Andropov (1982–84) Conservative former KGB chief who began anti-corruption and anti-alcohol campaigns but died shortly thereafter.

Konstantin Chernenko (1984–85) Described by *Newsweek* as Brezhnev's "chief pencil sharpener and bottle opener." Installed at age 73 to buy time for a scrambling Politburo.

Mikhail Gorbachev (1985–1991) Embarked on unprecedented reforms. He started a train he couldn't stop, though, and the USSR and his job ceased to exist while he was on vacation.

Boris Yeltsin (1991–2000) The first ever democratically elected ruler of Russia. Survived two coup attempts and tried to lift Russia out of the Third World. Ultimately lost his verve amidst multiple bypass surgeries, senility and Stolichnaya.

Vladimir Putin (2000–) Forty-seven-year-old former KGB spy force-fed to the electorate by Yeltsin. Makes people nervous by shamelessly consolidating presidential power.

RUSSIAN HISTORY AT A GLANCE

Sure it's foolhardy to condense one thousand years of intrigue into a few pages. But who's got time for the unabridged version?

9th Century

Vikings, called Varangians, leave Scandinavia to establish trading settlements with Slavs living in the Lake Ladoga and upper Volga regions. In 862 Norseman Rurik is "invited" to rule the Slavs' major northern settlement, which he calls Novgorod. The Russian state is born, as is the Rurik dynasty.

10th Century

Vladimir I introduces feudalism and the Eastern Orthodox religion. The Church establishes its base in Kiev. Novgorod breaks off from Kiev. The divided empire consists of numerous principalities, independently ruled and quasi-democratic although technically subservient to either Novgorod or Kiev.

11th Century

Kievan Rus enjoys a golden age under the rule of Yaroslav the Wise. The capital city is beautified on a Byzantine model. The first Russian metropolitan is appointed, symbolizing the Russian Orthodox Church's growing independence from Constantinople. In the north, Novgorod remains a powerful independent center of mercantilism and religion.

12th Century

Benevolent ruler Vladimir II Monomakh unites the empire for a brief period in the early century. He founds the city of Vladimir in the Rostov–Suzdal region, placing it under the rule of his son, Yury Dolgoruky. Under Yury Dolgoruky, the Rostov–Suzdal principality grows powerful, although the northern principalities, including Novgorod, once again splinter off. In an effort to expand and protect his domain, Yury founds the city of Moscow in 1147. The Church remains in Kiev.

13th Century

Mongols led by Genghis Khan thunder out of Asia and invade the Caucasus as well as the Volga and Don plains. They continue north and trounce the Russian princedoms until Genghis Khan suddenly dies. His grandson Batu Khan finishes the job with a vengeance, laying waste to every town from Kiev to Moscow. The Golden Horde, a khanate of the Mongol-Tatar empire, rules the Russian principalities until the 15th century from their base of Saray (near present day Volgograd) on the lower Volga. The Horde controls all local governments, appointing Russian princes to collect taxes. The Russians suffer a subjugation they never forget.

14th Century

The seat of the empire is moved to the Muscovy principality. Ivan I (the Moneybags), known for his energetic tax-collecting, is installed as grand prince. The Church also moves to Moscow. The Muscovy principality grows wealthy, as Ivan the Moneybags is also adept at embezzling. Later in the century Grand Prince Dmitry attacks the weakening Golden Horde, winning a historic battle at Kulikovo, on the Don River. The heroic grand prince earns the name Dmitry Donskoy (of the Don). The Golden Horde strikes back, however, violently ransacking the country true to form and enslaving nearly one million Russians.

15th Century

Under Vasily I and Vasily II, Muscovy continues to resist Mongol-Tatar domination. Ivan III (the Great) finally refuses to pay tribute to the Golden Horde, ending over two centuries of subjugation. Massive expansion follows. Ivan annexes major principalities, including Novgorod, to Muscovy and claims large portions of the Ural Mountains. The country at last stands more or less unified and five times larger than before Ivan's reign. The Russian Church becomes fully independent, and Moscow is declared the "third Rome," the true heir of Christianity. The city and Kremlin are rebuilt in a grand Byzantine style, and Muscovy adopts the former Byzantine crest of a double-headed eagle, which remains the symbol of the monarchy until 1917.

16th Century

Ivan III's grandson Ivan IV (the Terrible) is the first ruler to crown himself tsar of all Russia. Ivan conquers the once mighty Tatar strongholds of Kazan and Astrakhan, gaining the entire Volga region as well as access to the Caspian Sea and Siberia. In a fit of rage he kills his oldest son, Ivan, heir to the throne. Upon Ivan IV's death the throne is inherited by his second son, Fyodor I. Mentally slow, Fyodor is controlled by brother-in-law Boris Godunov, acting as regent. Boris Godunov allegedly orchestrates the murder of Fyodor's half-brother, Tsarevich Dmitry, in Uglich, setting the stage for his own uncontested ascension to the throne. Fyodor's death in 1598 marks the end of the Rurik dynasty, and Boris Godunov takes the throne.

17th Century

Widespread famine and peasant uprisings usher in the century and the Time of Troubles. In 1604, a Russian monk named Grigory living in Poland claims to be Tsarevich Dmitry, not murdered in Uglich after all. Discontented boyars as well as the Polish army back the pretender, who marches on Moscow. He kills Boris Godunov's son, who had taken the throne following Boris's death, and proclaims himself tsar. Known as False Dmitry I, he rules for a year before being overthrown and killed by a loyalist army led by boyar Vasily Shuisky, who takes the throne. Another pretender appears, and the Poles take advantage of the instability and occupy Moscow. Eventually a popular army led by Minin and Pozharsky evicts the Poles. In 1613 a young boyar named Michael Romanov is chosen by an assembly of the land to take the throne. The Time of Troubles ends; the 200-year-long Romanov dynasty begins.

Michael's successor, Alexey, makes large territorial gains, including the Ukraine and Siberia. He also turns serfs into slaves by proclaiming them unattached to their estates. Cossack Stepan Razin leads the country's largest ever peasant revolt, which ultimately is subdued. In 1689 Peter I (the Great) seizes power from his sister-regent, although he doesn't begin ruling with interest for another five years. Russia stands on the threshold of a new century and a remarkable reign.

18th Century

Peter the Great founds St. Petersburg in 1703, moving the capital there from Moscow nine years later. Peter force-feeds Western culture to Russia, fostering unprecedented advances as well as resentment. The country's first navy is instrumental in finally subduing the Swedes in the Northern War and gaining the Baltic territories.

After a series of relatively ineffectual rulers (Catherine I, Peter II, Anna, Ivan VI, Elizabeth, Peter III), the torch is passed to Catherine the Great, who continues to cultivate Western influences throughout Russia. The arts and sciences thrive like never before, although a newly formed class of critical elite begins to vocally oppose the monarchy. A Cossack named Pugachev leads the country's most violent peasant uprising but ends up captured and hanged. Various military campaigns result in the annexation of the Crimea, Lithuania and Byelorussia. Catherine's son Paul inherits the throne before the close of the century. He attempts to undo everything associated with Catherine but is murdered in an 1801 coup.

19th Century

Under Alexander I, Russia annexes Georgia, Azerbaijan and Finland. In 1812 Napoleon invades Russia, occupying Moscow. The city burns, but Alexander refuses to negotiate with Napoleon, forcing the French to retreat. They are chased back to Paris and ultimately surrender. Alexander's death in 1825 sparks a protest for reform staged by officers and aristocrats. Known as Decembrists, the protesters are subdued and either hanged or exiled by Alexander's successor, Nicholas I. Under his military-minded repressive rule, the country nonetheless enjoys economic growth.

Alexander II, son of Nicholas I, abolishes serfdom in 1861, although on terms that fail to appease the masses. A market economy and industrial expansion ensue, with urban working classes springing up in suburbs of major cities. Karl Marx's *Das Kapital* is translated into Russian, spawning Marxist groups, which take their place among other reform-minded factions. Russia sells Alaska to America for 7.2 million dollars. Alexander is assassinated in 1881, but the event fails to stir up the expected uprising. Alexander's son, Alexander III, rules for the next 13 years, repressing revolutionaries and escaping a major assassination attempt. Nicholas II, the last Russian tsar, takes the throne in 1894.

20th Century

Peaceful protesters are massacred by tsarist troops in a 1905 debacle called Bloody Sunday, egging on political discontent and social unrest. Workers councils called *soviets* are set up in St. Petersburg and Moscow. World War I drains the economy and absorbs Tsar Nicholas II, who steadily loses control over the people and abdicates in 1917. A democratically elected constituent assembly is formed. Lenin's Bolsheviks win a minority of seats and so forcefully dissolve the assembly, nipping representational government in the bud.

Lenin moves the capital of Russia back to Moscow, changing the name of the Bolshevik Party to the Communist Party. Foreign Affairs Minister Trotsky signs the Treaty of Brest, getting Russia out of WWI by ceding Finland, Poland, the Baltics, the Ukraine and the Caucasus. Civil war and famine rage through the country for the next three years, killing five million people. Russia is renamed the Union of Soviet Socialist Republics in 1922. Lenin dies two years later.

Josef Stalin outmaneuvers rivals and asserts supremacy as general secretary. Forced collectivization of all farms is implemented. Proliferation of heavy industry becomes the country's main goal, and Russia is transformed from a floundering agricultural nation to a global industrial leader. Stalin purges party members, military leaders and intellectuals—millions are executed or sent to labor camps. World War II costs the USSR 25 million lives but gains it the Ukraine and Baltic States and dominance throughout eastern Europe. The Cold War begins, and purges continue. The final death toll of Stalin's reign of terror is 30 million. The most murderous dictator the world has ever known dies in 1953.

Nikita Khrushchev takes power and denounces Stalin. The country enjoys a brief intellectual and cultural thaw. The Cuban missile crisis, rift with China, economic failure and other setbacks cost Khrushchev his job in 1964. Under Khrushchev's successor, Leonid Brezhnev, the Soviet

Union invades Czechoslovakia in 1968 and Afghanistan in 1979. Repressions continue, and economic stagnation plagues the country. Brezhnev dies in 1982. Former KGB chief Yury Andropov succeeds Brezhnev but dies three years later. Konstantin Chernenko steps in for less than a year before kicking the bucket in 1985.

Fifty-four year-old Mikhail Gorbachev emerges as general secretary. Championing a new style of leadership, he aims to revive the economy and make peace with the West. He introduces *glasnost* (openness) and *perestroika* (restructuring). Political prisoners and exiles, including Nobel laureate Andrey Sakharov, are freed. Boris Yeltsin becomes parliamentary chairman. He tears up his Communist Party card and proclaims independence of the Russian state, mimicking gestures already made by the Baltic republics. A failed coup attempt by Party hard-liners in August 1991 results in the dissolution of the Communist Party and the collapse of the Soviet Union.

Boris Yeltsin gains control of the Russian government. Gorbachev officially steps down four months later. Yeltsin's goal is to introduce full-blown democracy and capitalism. Privatization of state enterprises commences. Ill-prepared for a free market system, the post-Soviet economy worsens. In September 1993 Yeltsin dissolves Parliament, calling for free elections. In December the first truly multi-party elections are held for Parliament, and the Russian Constitution, including a Bill of Rights, is ratified. In 1996 Yeltsin is elected for the first time as president of Russia. Somewhat of a lame duck because of an antagonistic parliament, degenerating health, senility and a penchant for drink, Yeltsin fails to live up to expectations.

Former KGB spy Vladimir Putin is hand-picked by Yeltsin to succeed him. Unsurprisingly, Putin is elected president in 2000. Adept at modern politics, he placates the West while consolidating presidential power at home, revoking regional gubernatorial elections, keeping televised media in his back pocket and banishing potential political threats, such as billionaire oligarch Mikhail Khodorkovskiy, to Siberia, using the Russian court system, clearly also under presidential control.

SOUVENIR BUYING GUIDE

Each port of call chapter in this book concludes with advice on products and handicrafts that are native to that particular city or region. Here is a more general rundown of the souvenirs and collectibles you can acquire just about anywhere and anytime during your trip.

Unfortunately, the days of using American cigarettes as currency or engaging in profitable bartering with your own T-shirts or blue-jeans are long gone in Russia. It is a normalized market now, and like most other places in the world, money talks loudest. Technically, businesses in Russia are prohibited from selling goods for foreign currencies, although it is doubtful that a souvenir vendor, especially in the provinces, is going to lose a sale by refusing dollars or euros.

In terms of how to spend your money, prices on the streets and at flea markets tend to be better than in tourist shops. However, shops can offer good deals on items not available on the streets. Western hotels naturally ask the most exorbitant prices for souvenirs and other goods but offer the advantage of accepting credit cards and stocking high quality merchandise.

The souvenir kiosk on your ship is a recommended place to shop because it likely offers competitive prices, a thoughtful selection and unbeatable convenience. With that said, if your ship's gift shop is selling copies of *Russia by River* that don't bear the same cover as this one, then it is engaging in piracy, and you are discouraged from patronizing it.

In general, if something strikes your fancy, buy it. You might pass up a lot of appealing things during the cruise in hopes of doing better at your final destination of either Moscow or St. Petersburg only to end up short on time once there. If you buy a painted tray in Uglich only to find the identical tray in Moscow for a few hundred rubles less, so what? And if you find a much nicer lacquer box in St. Petersburg than the one you already bought back in Yaroslavl, you can always give the bad one to Aunt Myrtle, and she will love it.

Painted lacquer boxes

Because lacquer boxes range from cheap trinkets to valuable pieces of art, it is important to know how to distinguish an authentic from a fake, because well-crafted boxes can sit right next to bad imitations.

Genuine hand-painted boxes come from only four villages in Russia: Palekh, Fedoskino, Mstera and Kholui. The name of the village as well as that of the artist (both in Cyrillic) should be painted on the box itself. Each village is known for its distinct manner of painting. Artists from Palekh are renowned for using gold leaf in rendering highly detailed and intricate scenes on a rich black background. Fedoskino painters incorporate mother of pearl either in their pigments or directly on their boxes. The trademark Fedoskino scene is a tea party, depicting two bearded men at a table with a samovar. Mstera artisans make liberal use of blue tones, which make their painting distinctly colorful. Painters from Kholui tend to render their scenes in a comparatively flat manner.

There are two main types of impostor boxes. The first actually are not painted at all, but instead bear a print touched up with paint. The second are simply poorly executed by untrained artists not hailing from one of the above-mentioned villages. Using a magnifying glass (often furnished by respectable dealers) is the best way to judge a box's quality. Questions to ask yourself include the following: Does the scene look like it was clipped from a magazine and pasted onto the box? Is the brushwork meticulous or sloppy? Are the designs or scenes on the sides of the box rendered in the same style as that of the picture on top? Do the pieces of the box fit together properly? Is it really a paper mâché box, or is it plastic?

Many excellent boxes are collectors items and fetch thousands of dollars. Others that are indeed well done and genuine can be had for thirty to sixty dollars. Minuscule boxes are often more expensive than larger ones simply because of the skill required to paint on them. Boxes with painting on all sides are naturally more expensive than those painted only on top. If you're looking at a box as an investment, be absolutely certain of its authenticity. If you want a simple memento, don't worry so much, for even crude fakes can exhibit a desirable charm.

Matryoshka dolls

The ubiquitous Russian nesting dolls called *matryoshki* are a mandatory purchase. Although the guidelines for identifying quality ones are not as involved as those for lacquer boxes, most of the same rules apply. Simply inspect the craftsmanship. The more skillfully painted the dolls, the more valuable they are. And naturally the more dolls to a set, the more costly it is. Look for especially good sets in Mandrogi.

Chess

Even if you're no Gary Kasparov, a Russian chess set makes a wonderful acquisition. Although few sets are genuine pieces of art, the majority are delightfully colorful and playfully painted. The big thing to look out for is the material used, which ought to be wood. Even if the board and all the pieces seem to be made of wood, double check the knights, which are often painted-over plastic molds. Occasionally you can find exquisite chess sets made in Russian-Asian republics such as Kirghizia. These sets are meticulously painted and carved and utilize a variety of exotic wood. They're comparatively expensive, but usually worth far more than what you pay.

Timepieces

There is certainly no Rolex equivalent in Russia, but a variety of unique and reliable timepieces are available. Mechanically speaking, three types of watches are available: quartz, automatic and wind-up. Quartz watches can't be wound; automatic watches are wound by wrist movement; and wind-up watches are, well, wound by twisting the knob. Although a novelty to the Swatch generation, the latter variety represents your best bet. It can be a problem replacing the battery of a Russian quartz watch at home, and automatic watches are the most prone to break. A good old-fashioned wind-up, however, can last you a lifetime.

The most popular Russian watches are those made by the Chaika factory in Uglich and the clunky yet undeniably hip Russian military watches. Chaikas are known by there enamel bands and make wonderful gifts for ladies. For men, stick with the military watches, which have

17-jewel movement and are waterproof to fifty meters. Their faces come in a variety of colors and styles and bear a small emblem of either a tank, a submarine, a parachute, a ship, a jet or a red star.

Caviar

Buying caviar in Russia can be an art in itself. Aficionados who know the difference between the three main varieties (*osetra*, *sevruga* and *beluga*) will seek out local markets and fish shops. Everybody else must decide what to do with all those tins and jars offered by the kids at the side of the ship. Here is the answer: do not buy any caviar that has not been kept refrigerated since its original packaging. Real caviar, which comes only from sturgeons, spoils if it is not kept constantly cool. If you're after real caviar in good condition, forget about buying it on the streets. If you don't care so much about the condition of the eggs, go ahead and buy caviar off the street, as it is entirely edible but dried-out and lumpy. If you have friends at home who won't know the difference between dried-out and well-kept caviar, you may as well buy a few gifts.

Red caviar technically is not caviar at all, as it comes from salmon. It is, however, cheaper than black and quite tasty. It is not nearly as fragile, so you can get away with buying it just about anywhere.

If you want to experience the real thing while in Russia, you'll have to buy your caviar from a bar, restaurant or shop. And you'll have to eat it while in Russia, as you won't be able to get it home without spoiling it. If you want to look like a connoisseur, forget the bread, the crackers, the chopped onions and the sour cream, and eat your caviar with nothing but a mother-of-pearl spoon.

Vodka

Russian vodka is more durable than caviar, although there are many impostor brands, some of which are pure lighter fluid. Following a few simple buying guidelines will allow you to taste for yourself the acclaimed spirit that gets the Russians through their Arctic winters.

Many foreign vodkas have invaded the Russian market to cater to the vast majority of Russians who believe that anything produced outside their country, including their famed national spirit, is superior to the native-made product. Imported brands often have Russian-sounding names, so you are recommended to stick to these established Russian brands: Stolichnaya, Russkaya, Moskovskaya, Pyatizvezdochnaya (five star), Pertsovka (pepper-flavored), Limonnaya (lemon-flavored) and Pshenichnaya (wheat vodka). One of the most popular luxury brands that still has not made it to the States is the handsomely bottled Russky Standart.

To be like a real Russian, drink your vodka from a *ryumka* (shot glass) and in one gulp. Proposing a toast before each shot is mandatory, no matter how many rounds you have. The standard toast is *na zdoroviye* or *za zdoroviye* ("to your health"). You can get more original by inserting anything you want after the *za* ("to"). Thus other variants might be *za kapitana* ("to the captain") or for those trying to make time with the pretty onboard guides, *za dam* ("to the ladies").

Other beverages

Local beers and brandies are great gifts, if you don't mind the extra weight in your luggage. The most popular brand of beer in all of Russia is the St. Petersburg-based Baltika, which produces nine grades of their pasteurized brew. The higher the number, the stronger. Russian brandies, to the chagrin of the French, are often called cognacs, although in no way are they related to the real thing. Georgian cognac is better than Russian, and Armenian is considered the *crème de la crème* of eastern European brandies. Russian wines are hopeless, although some sweet Georgian wines can be interesting to the collector.

INDEX